COLORED HORSE'S

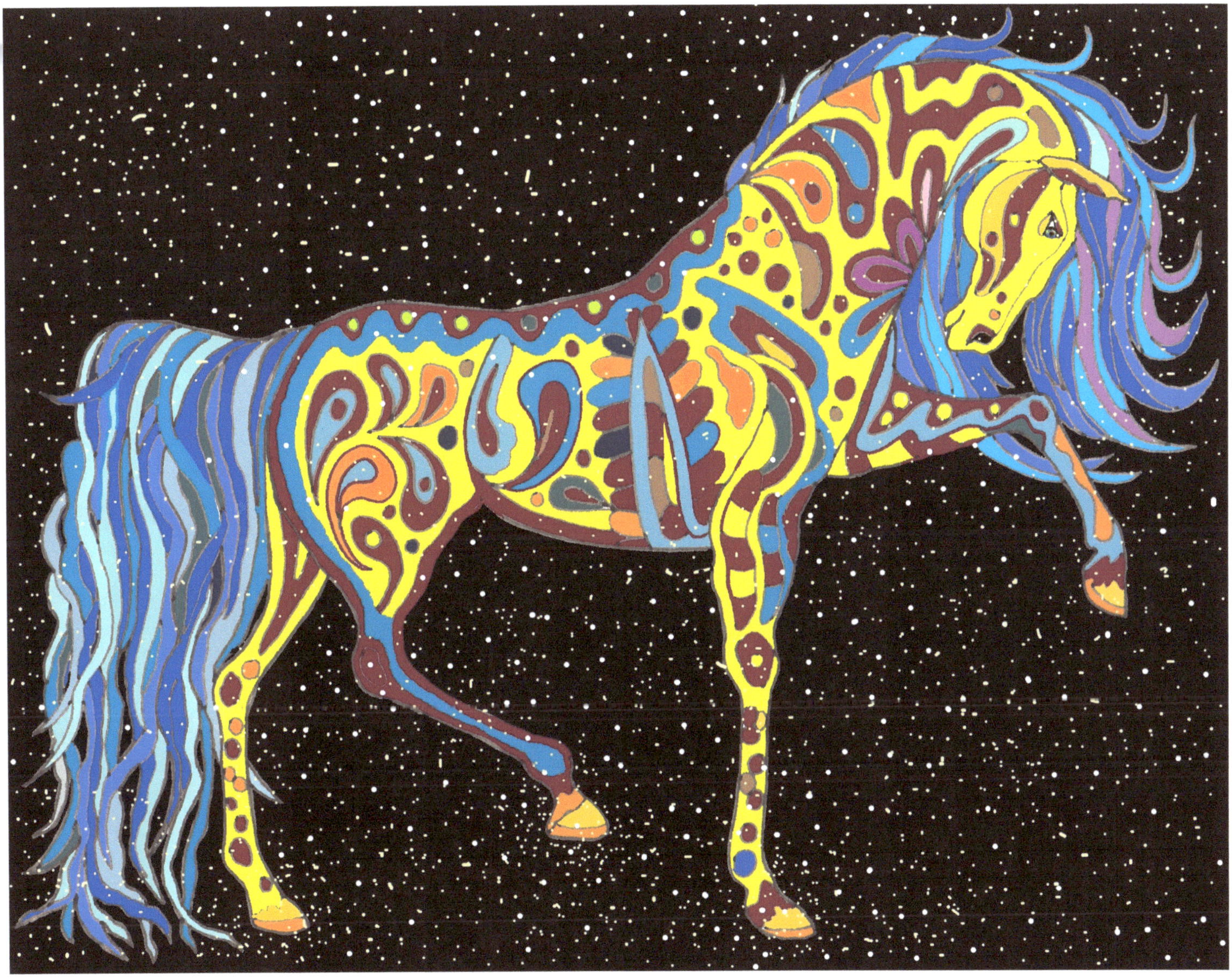

Colored Horse's Coloring Book for Adults & Children

Copyrights 2018© Lauri Ann Kraft

All rights reserved

Permission to post copies of my artwork
online as part of a book review.

WWW.COLORWYOMING.COM

WWW.FACEBOOK.COM/KRAFTSART

ISBN-13: 978-1986671743

Colorful Coloring

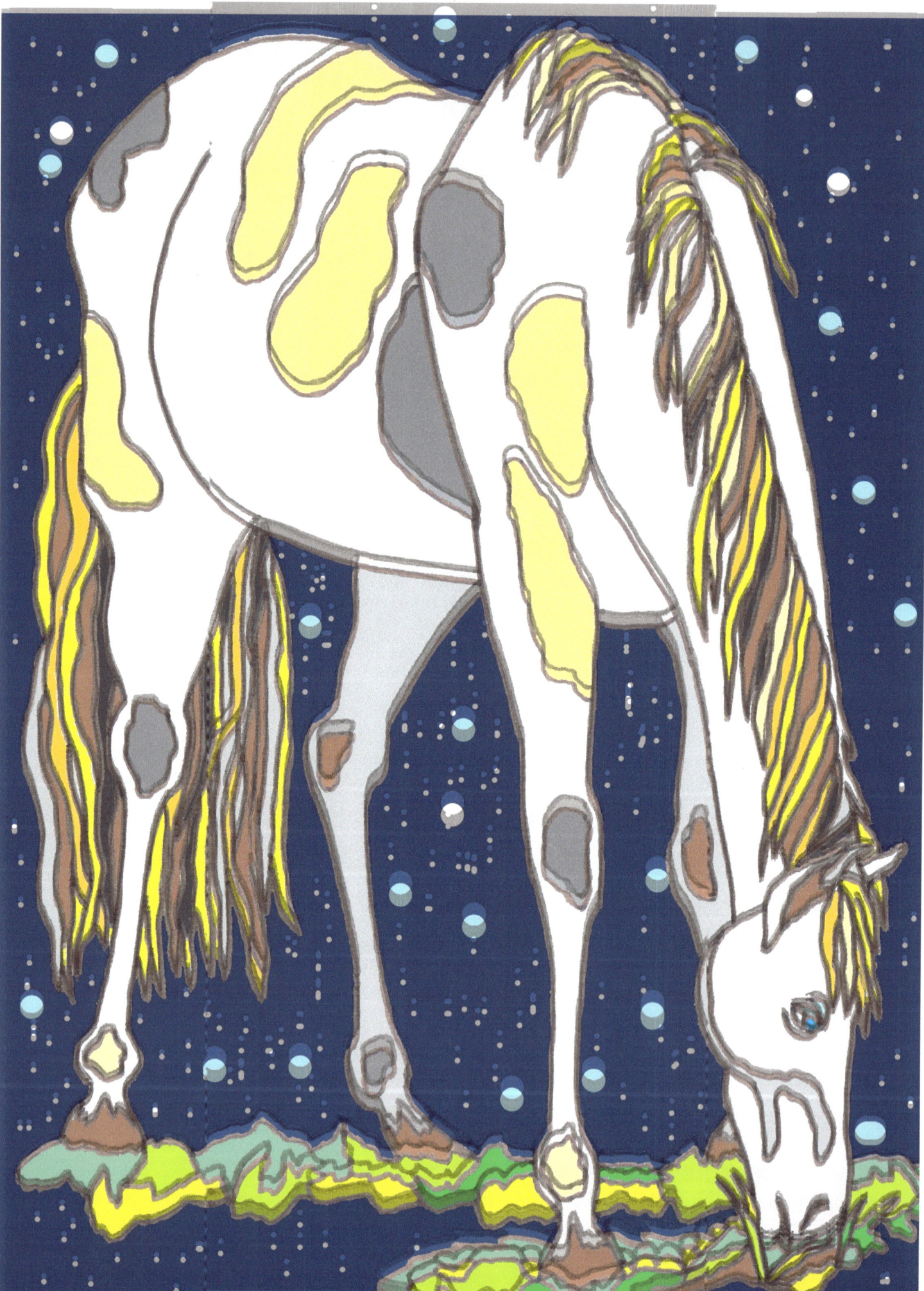

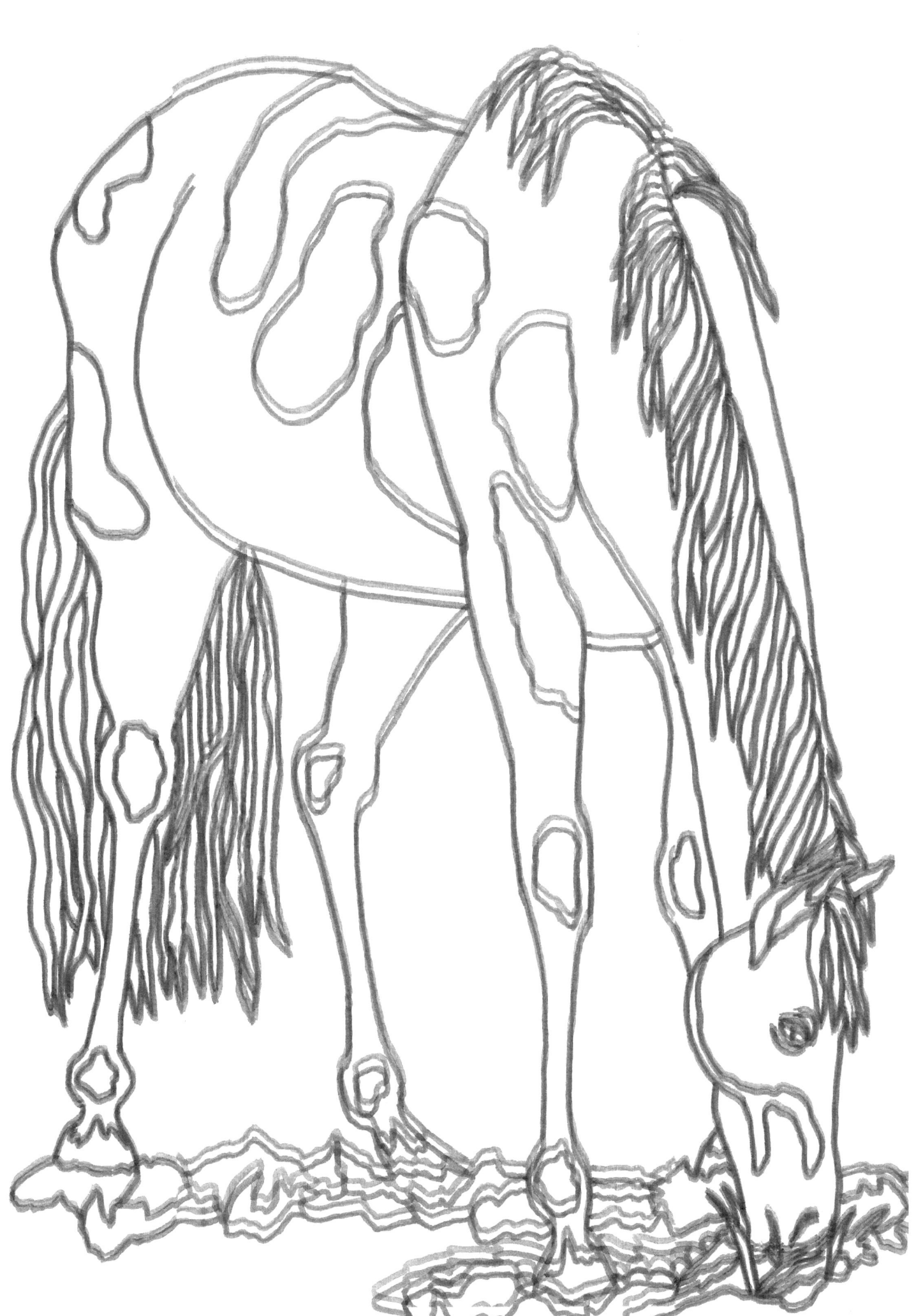

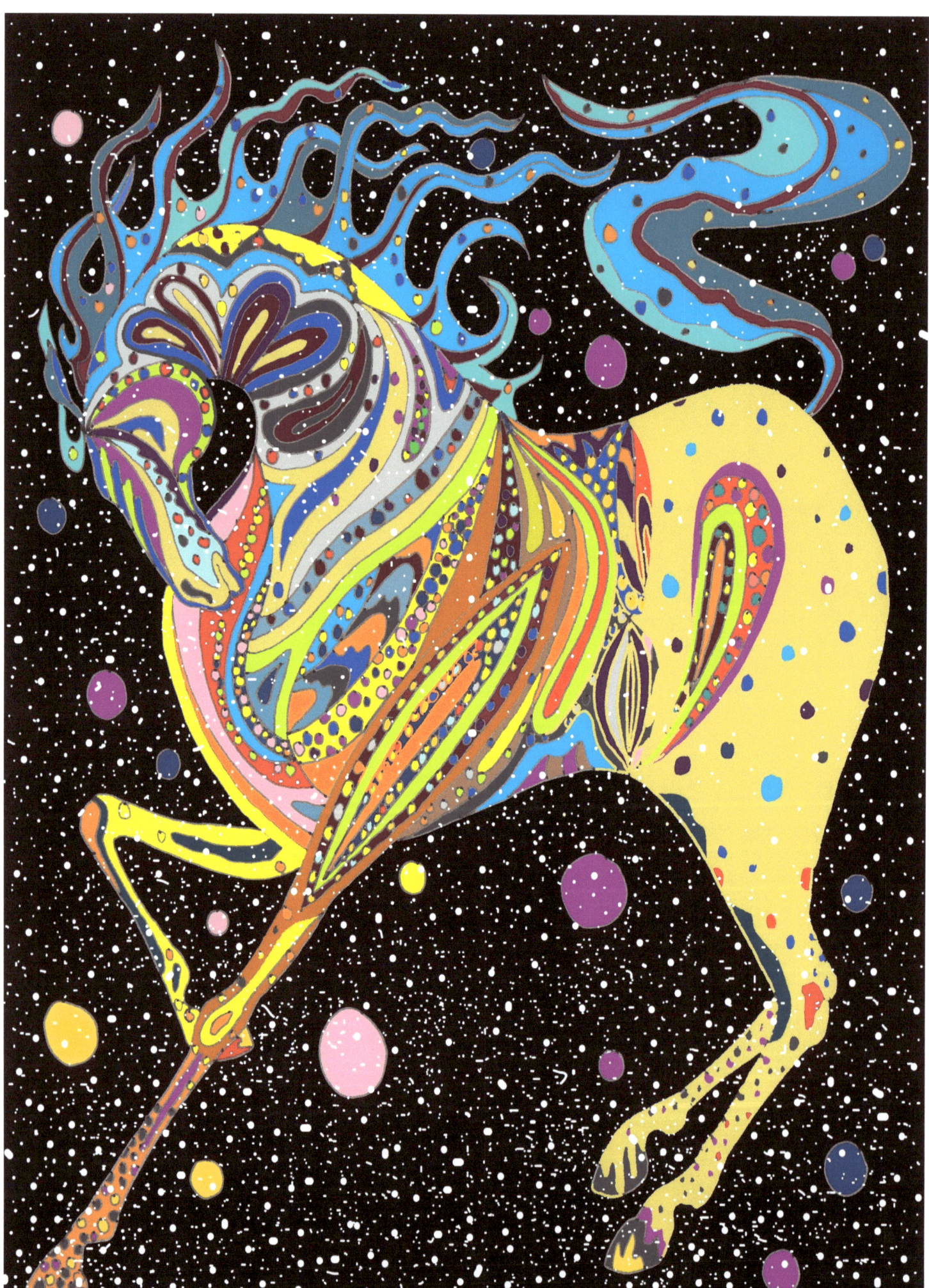

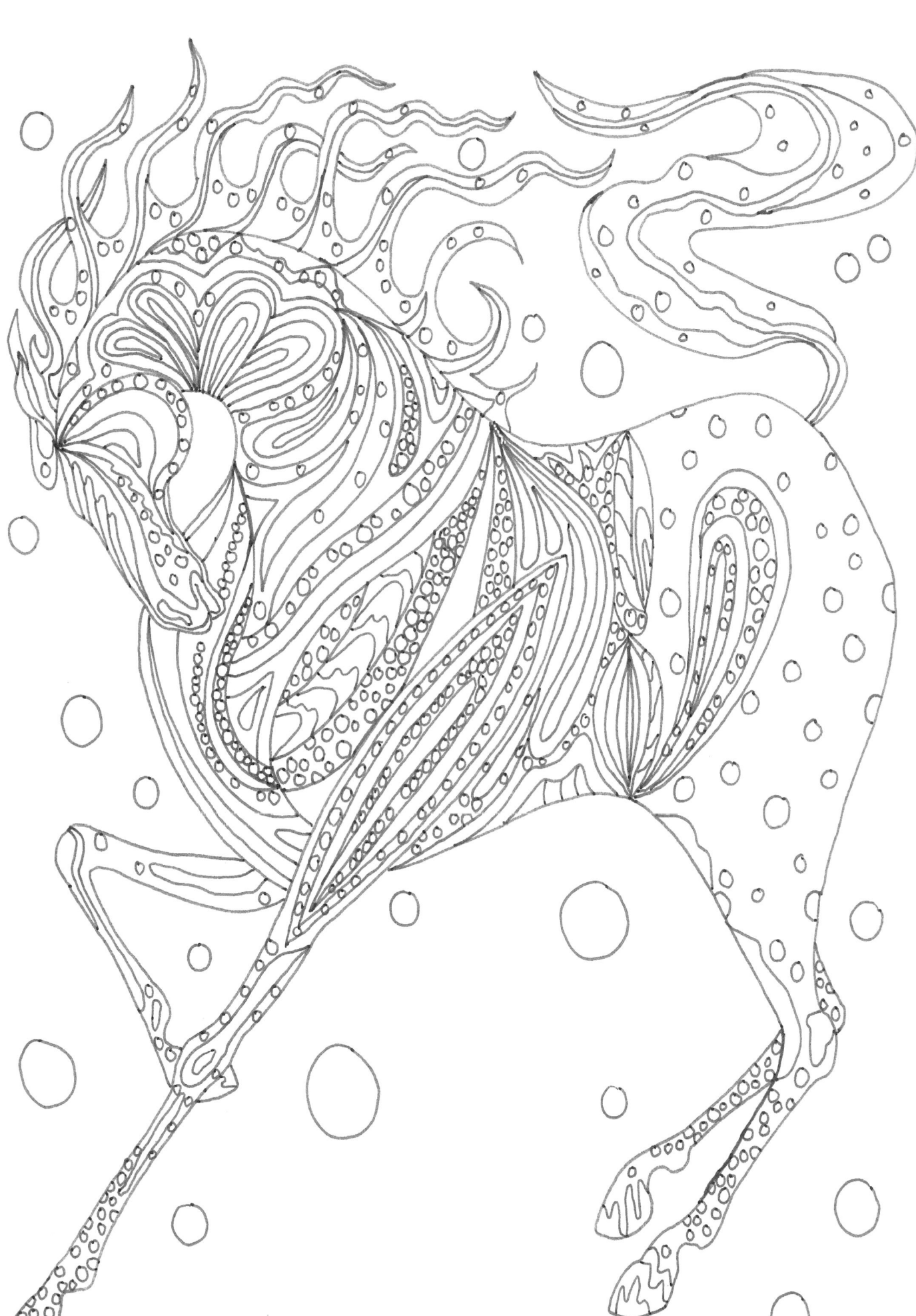

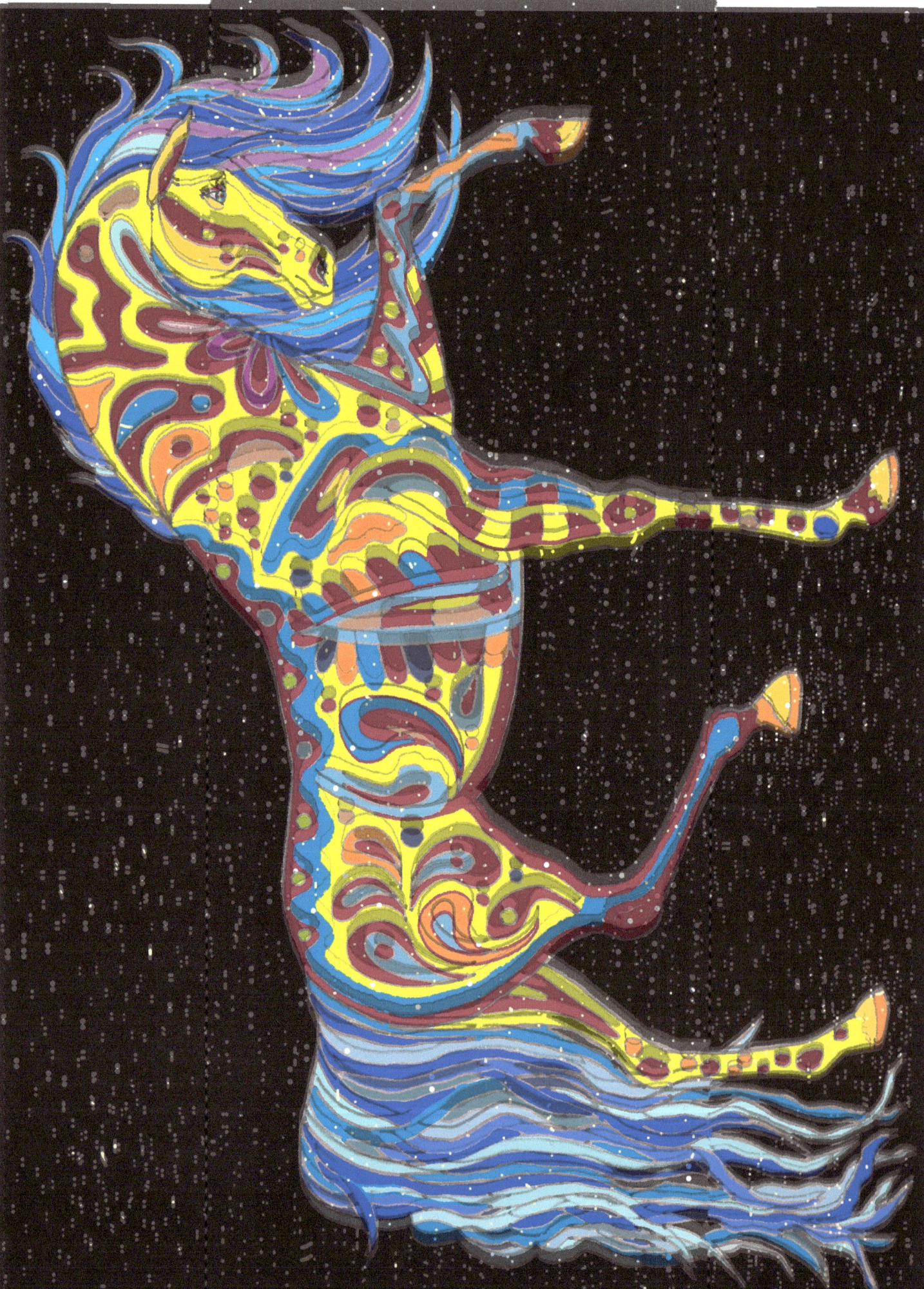

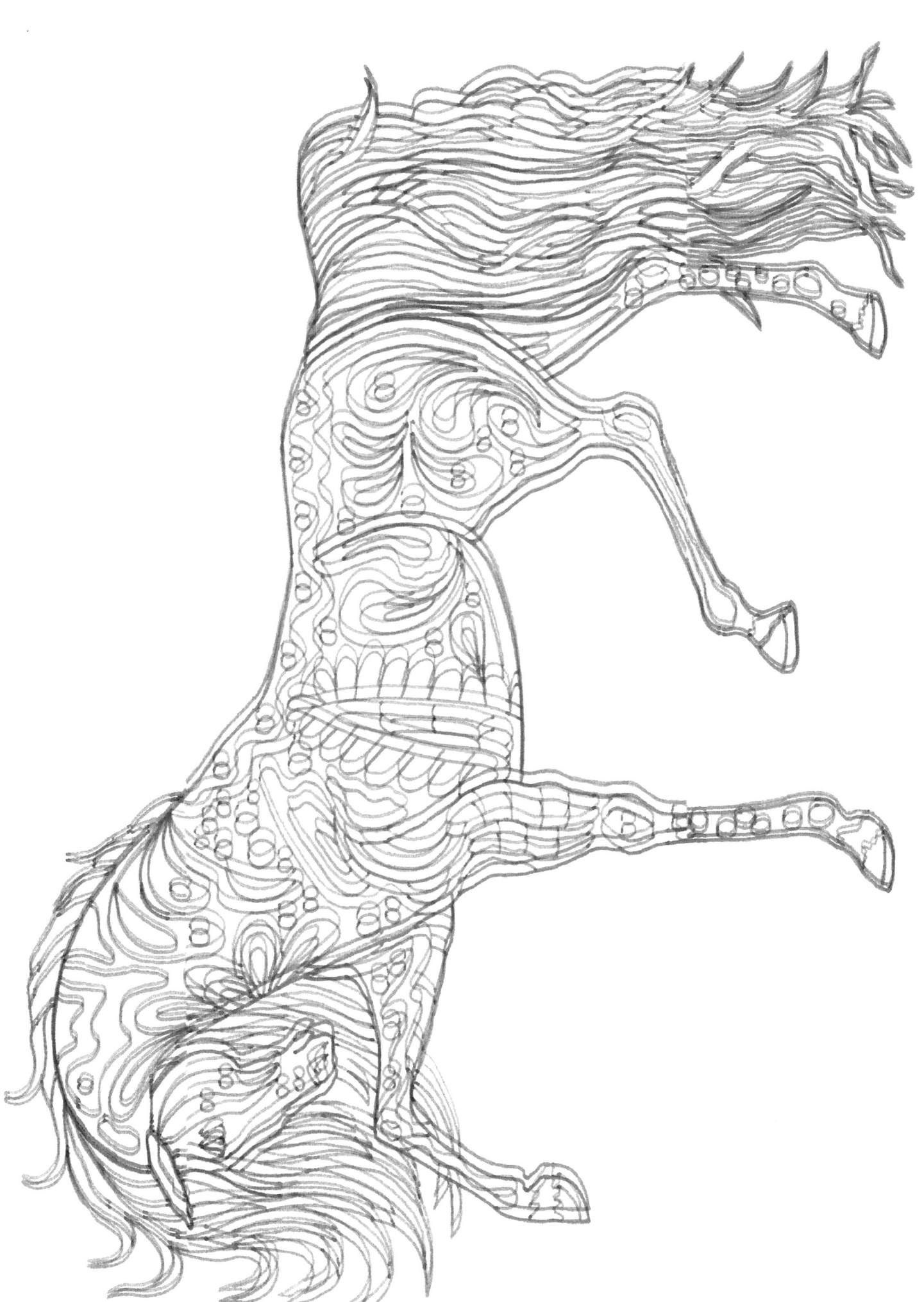

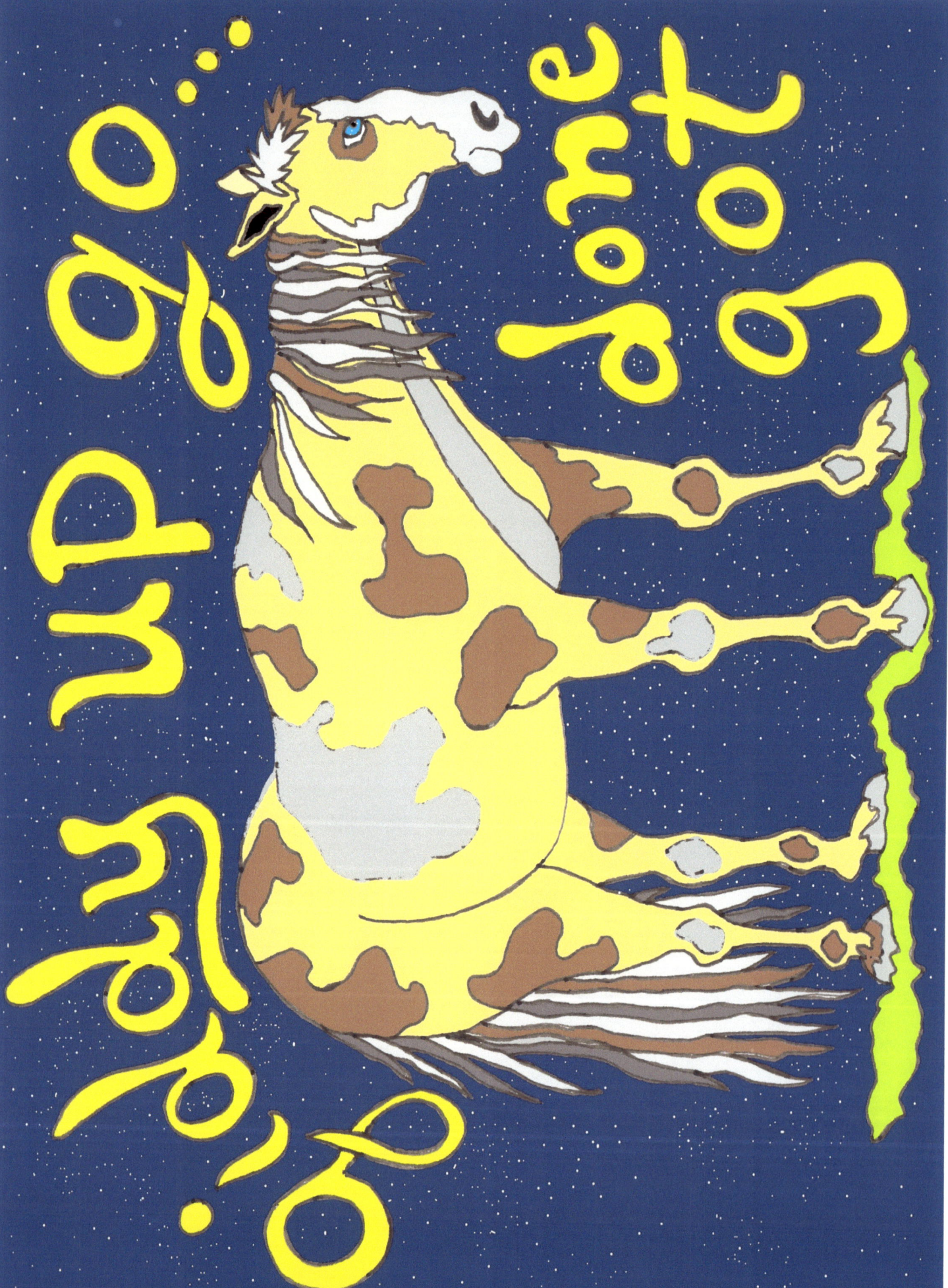

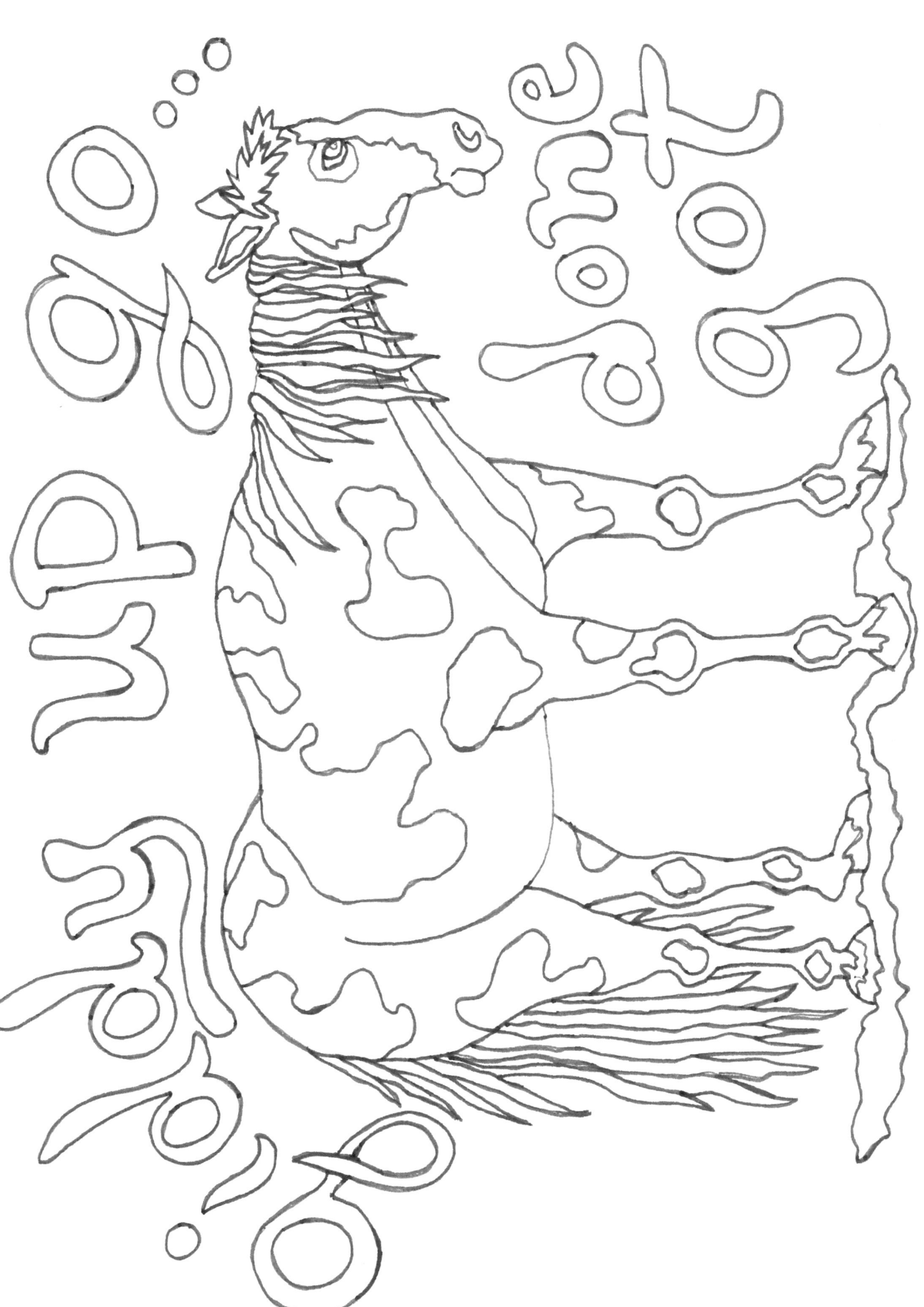

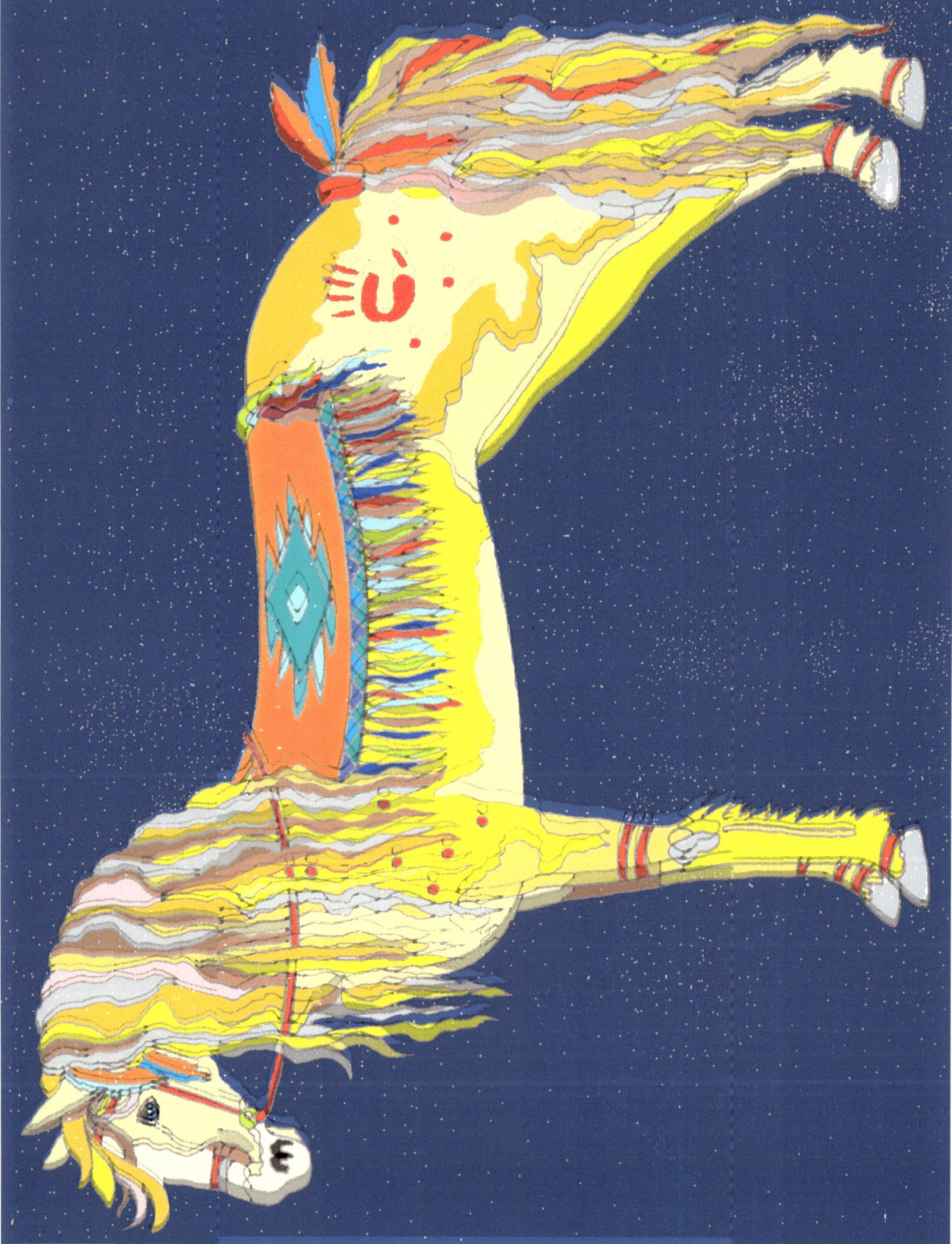

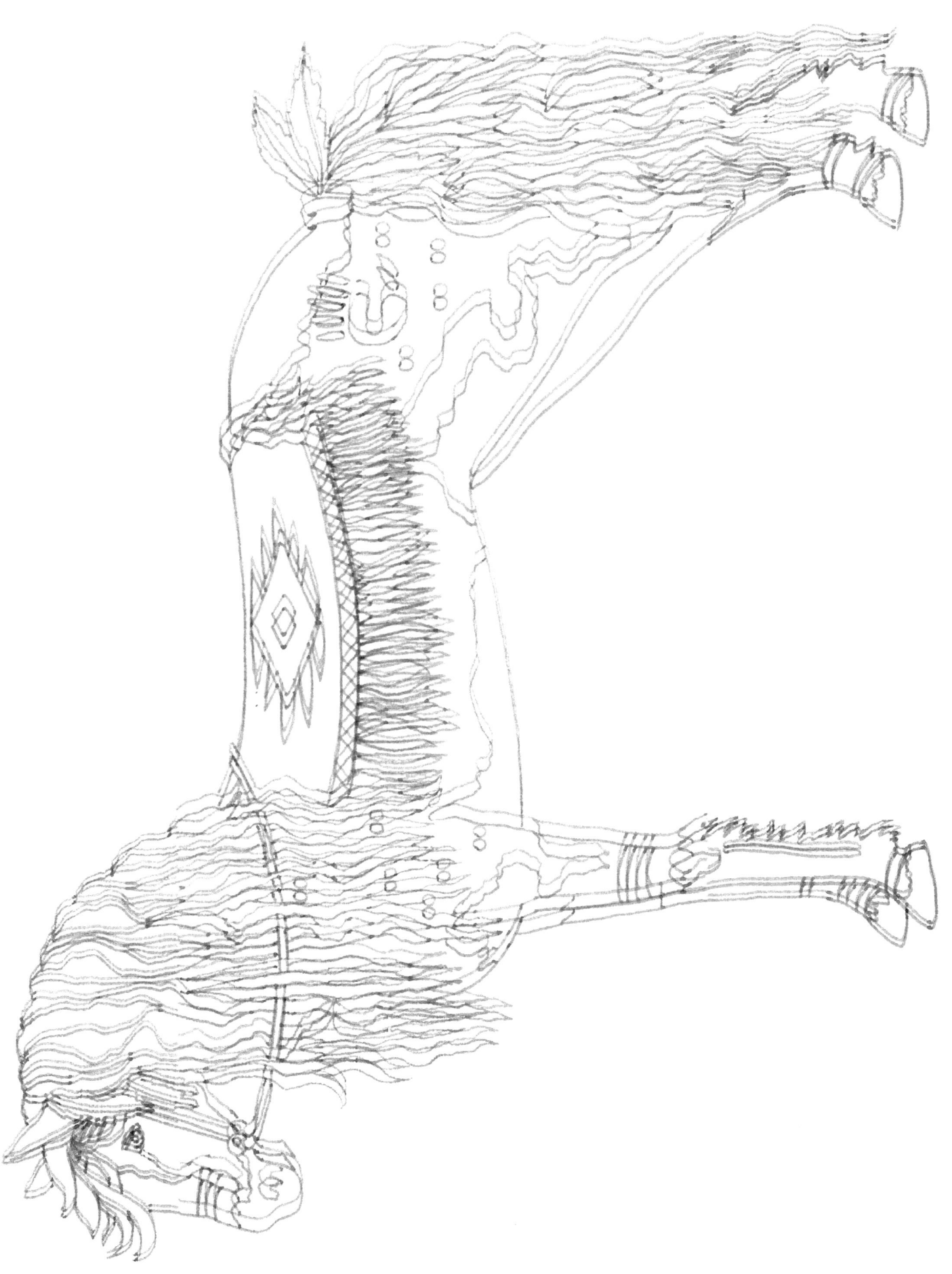

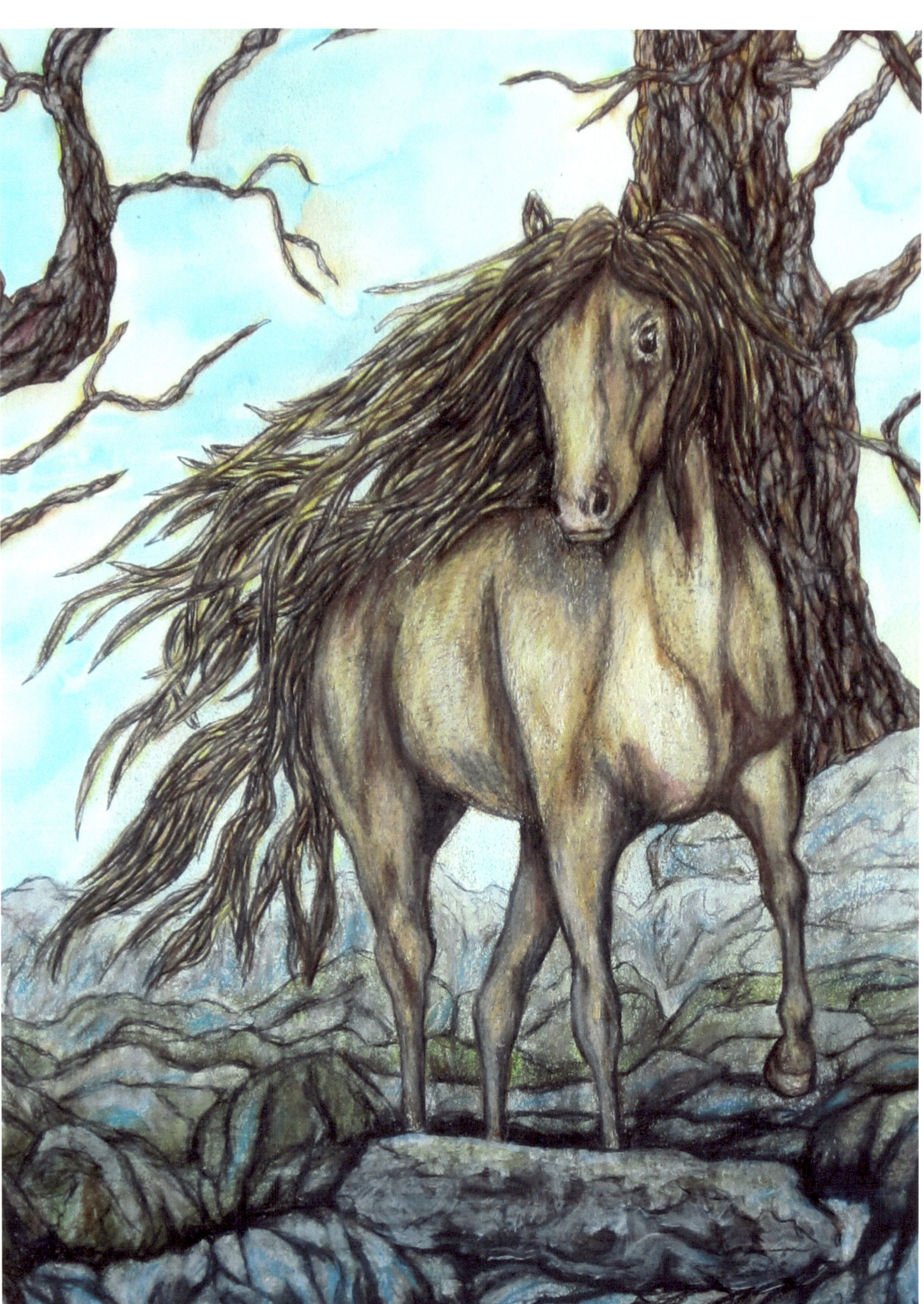

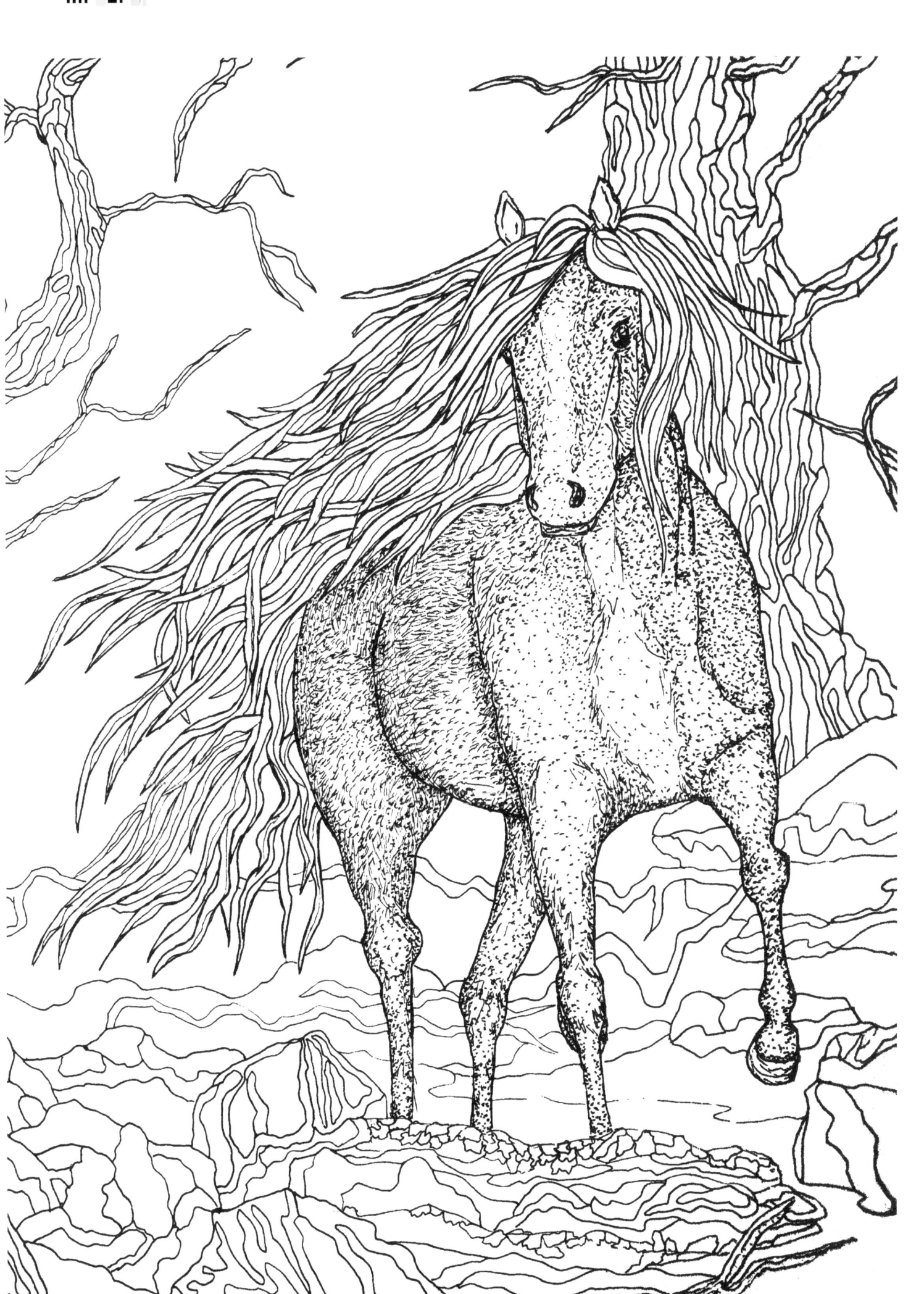

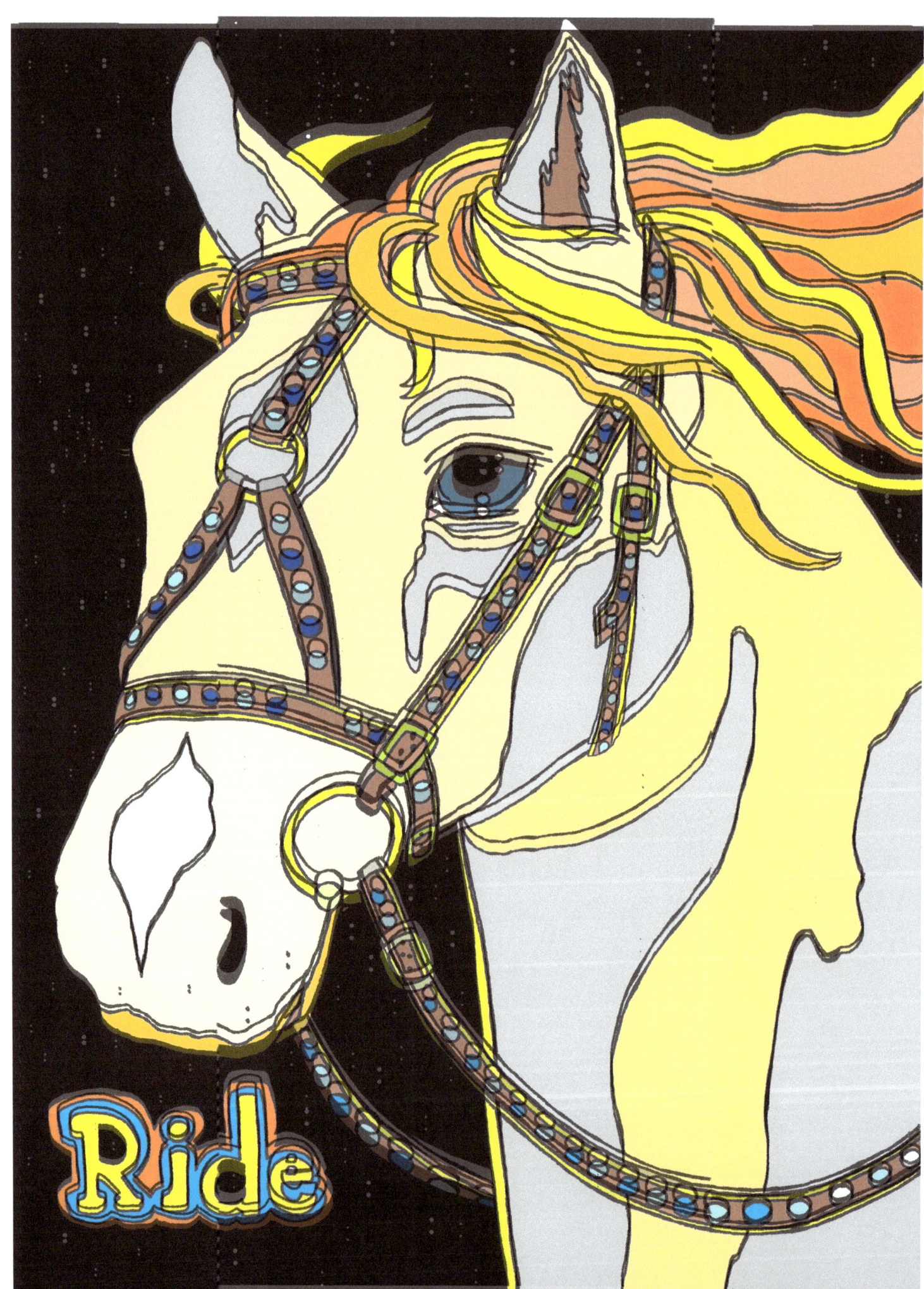

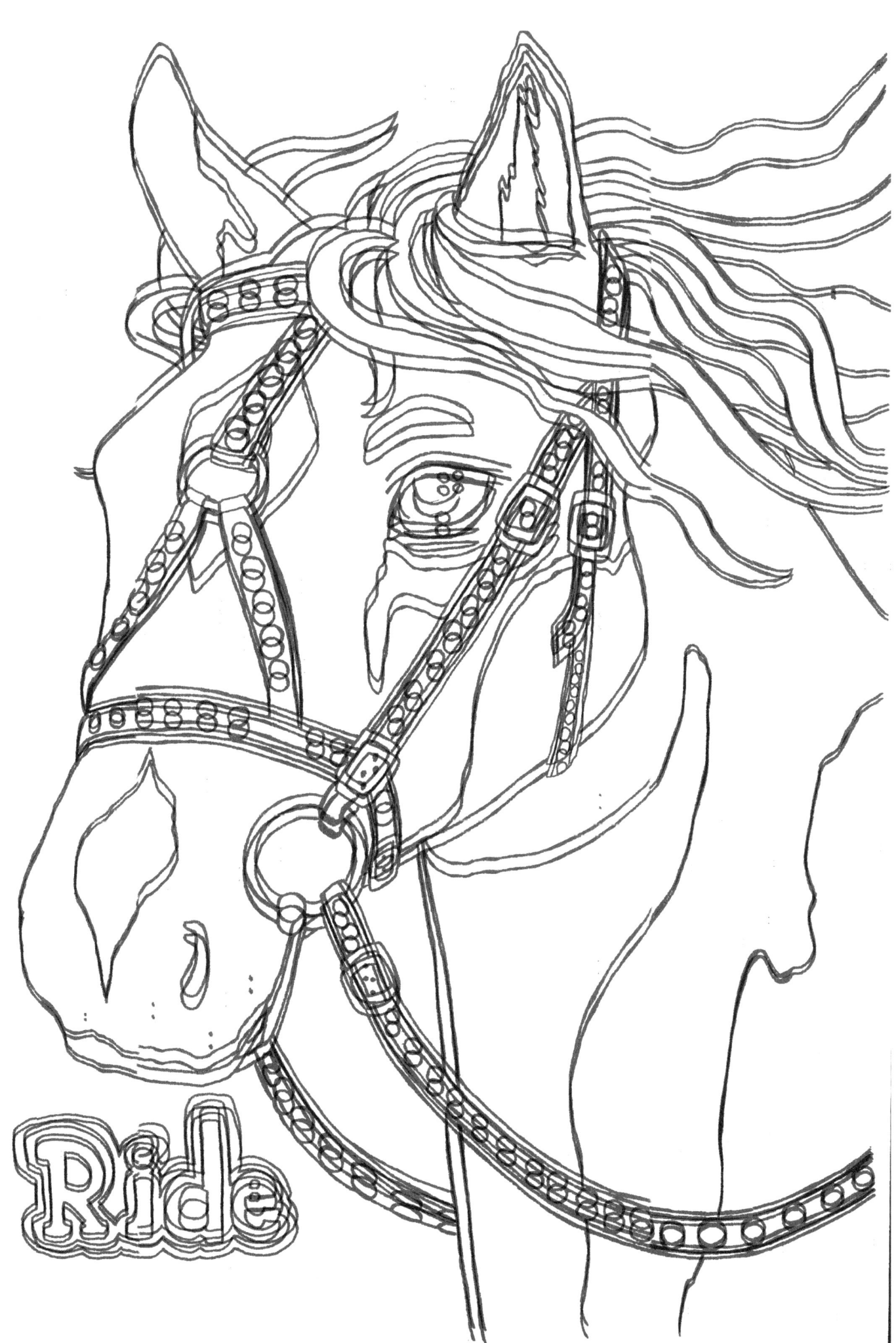

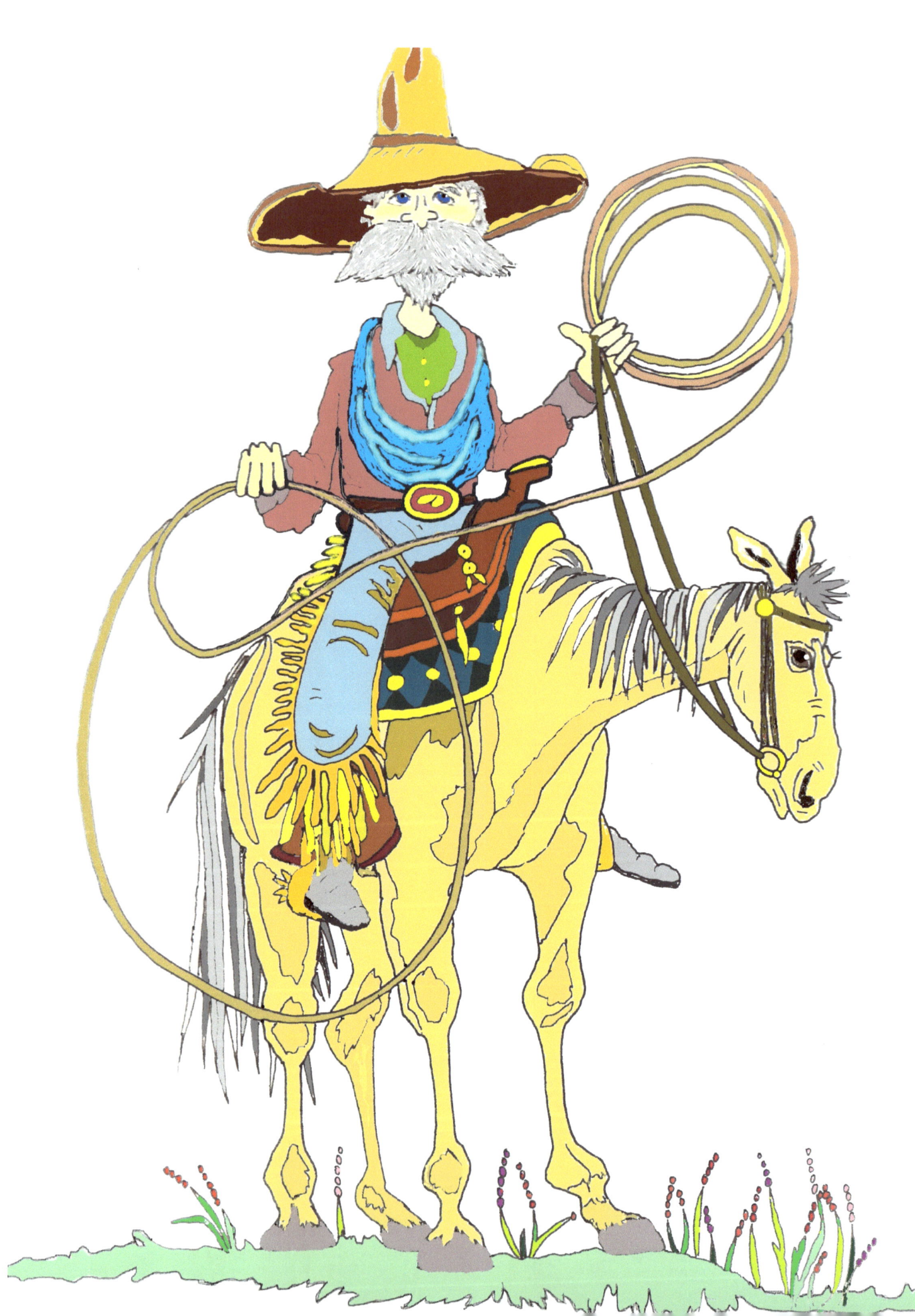

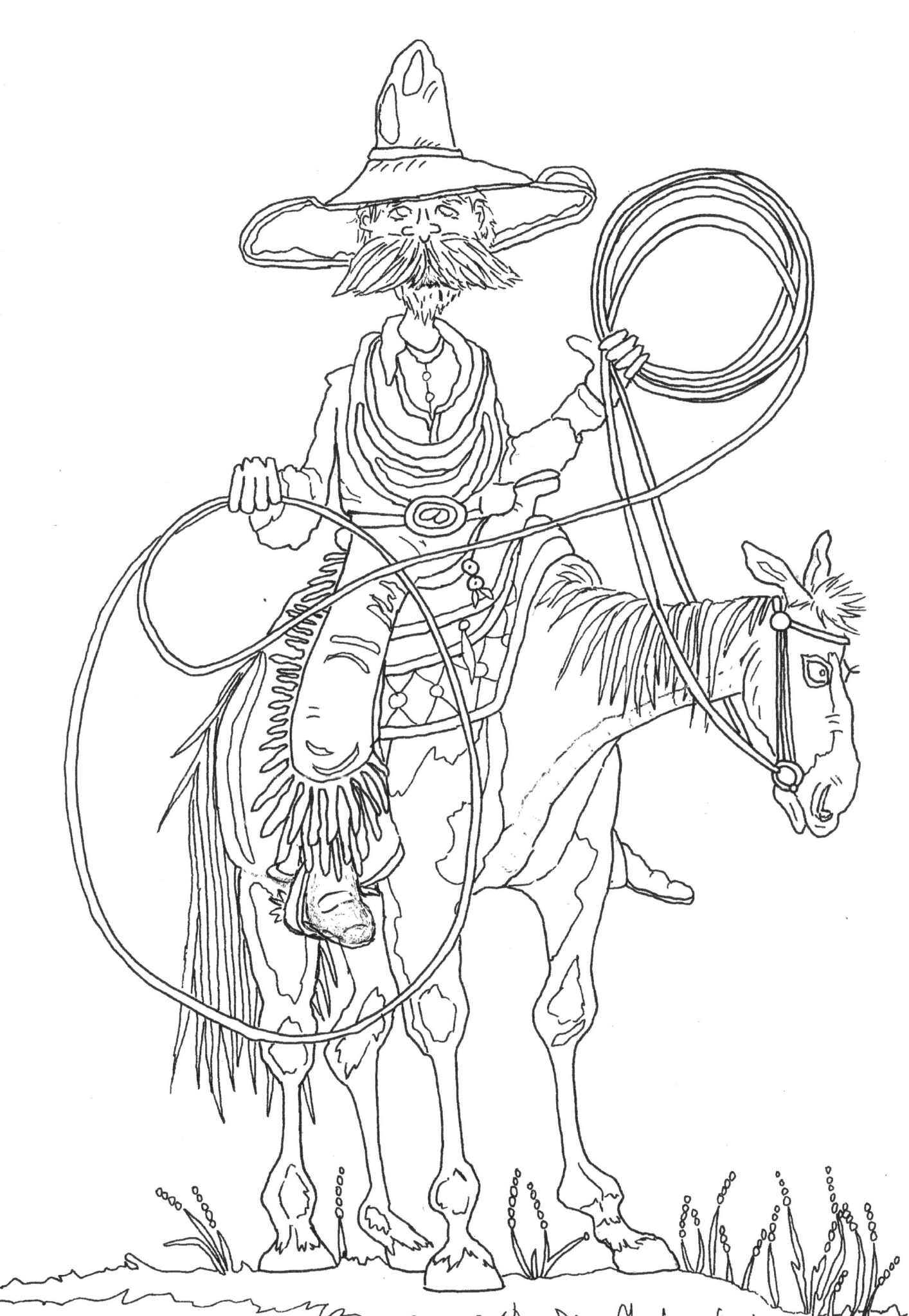

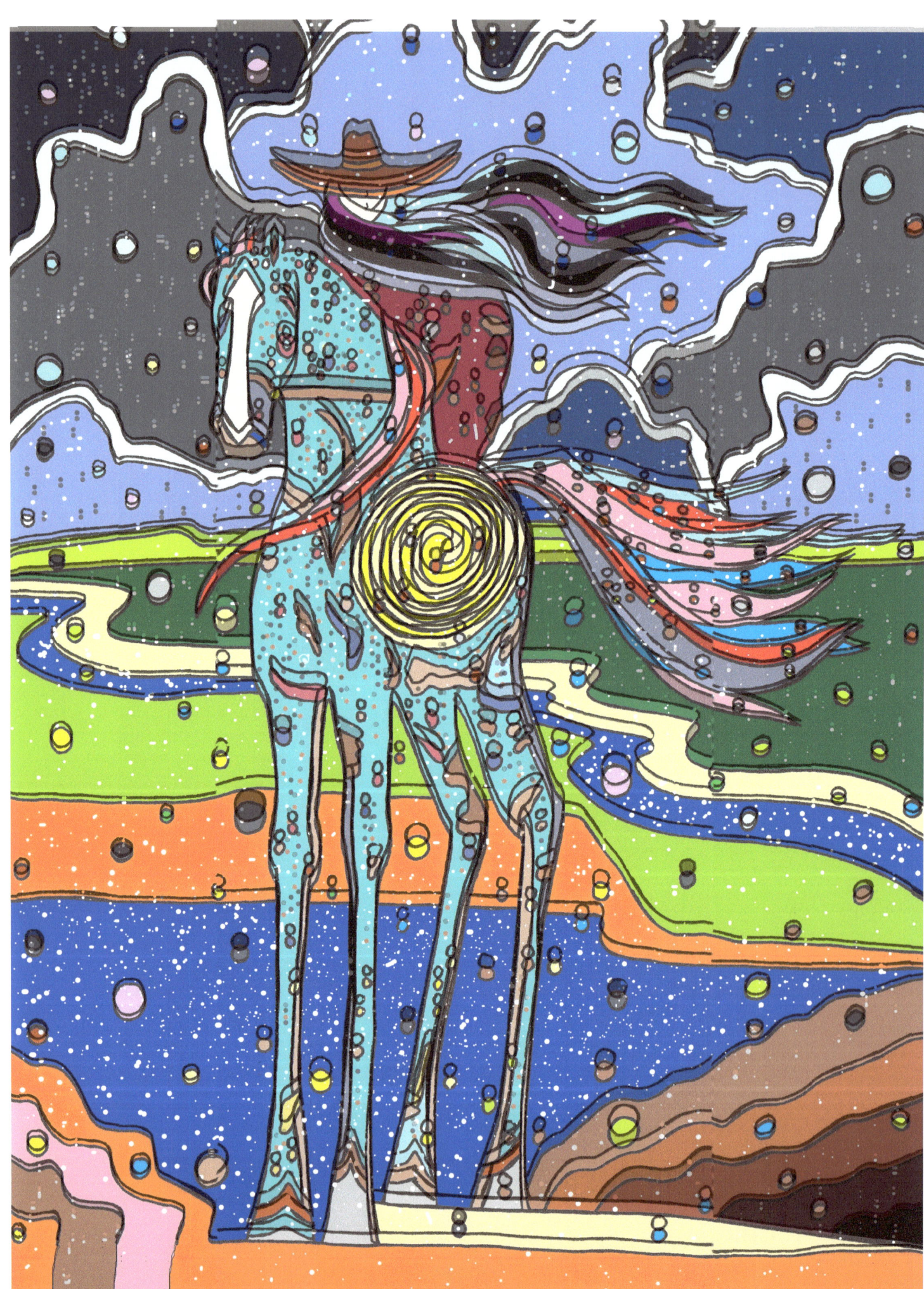

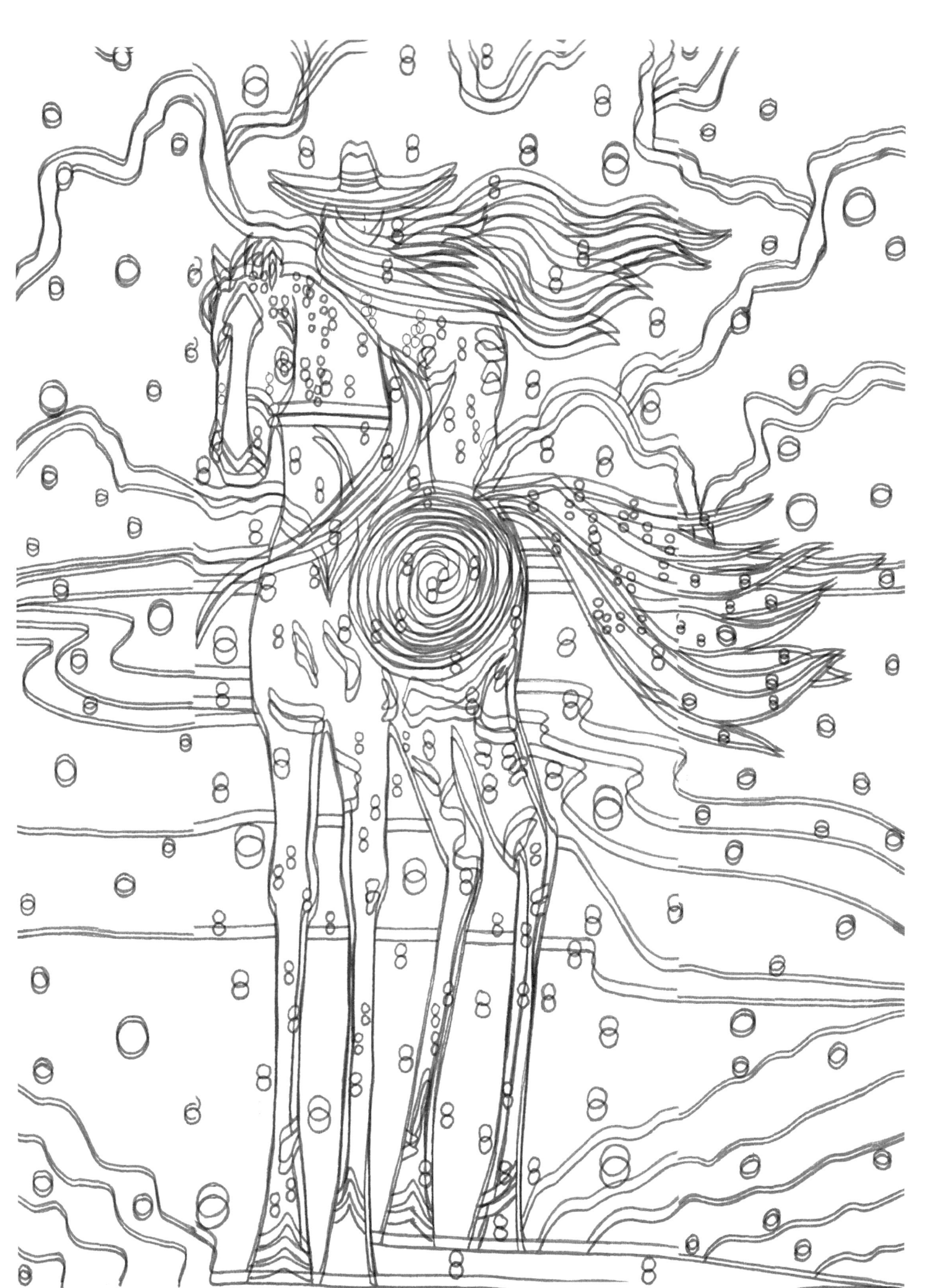

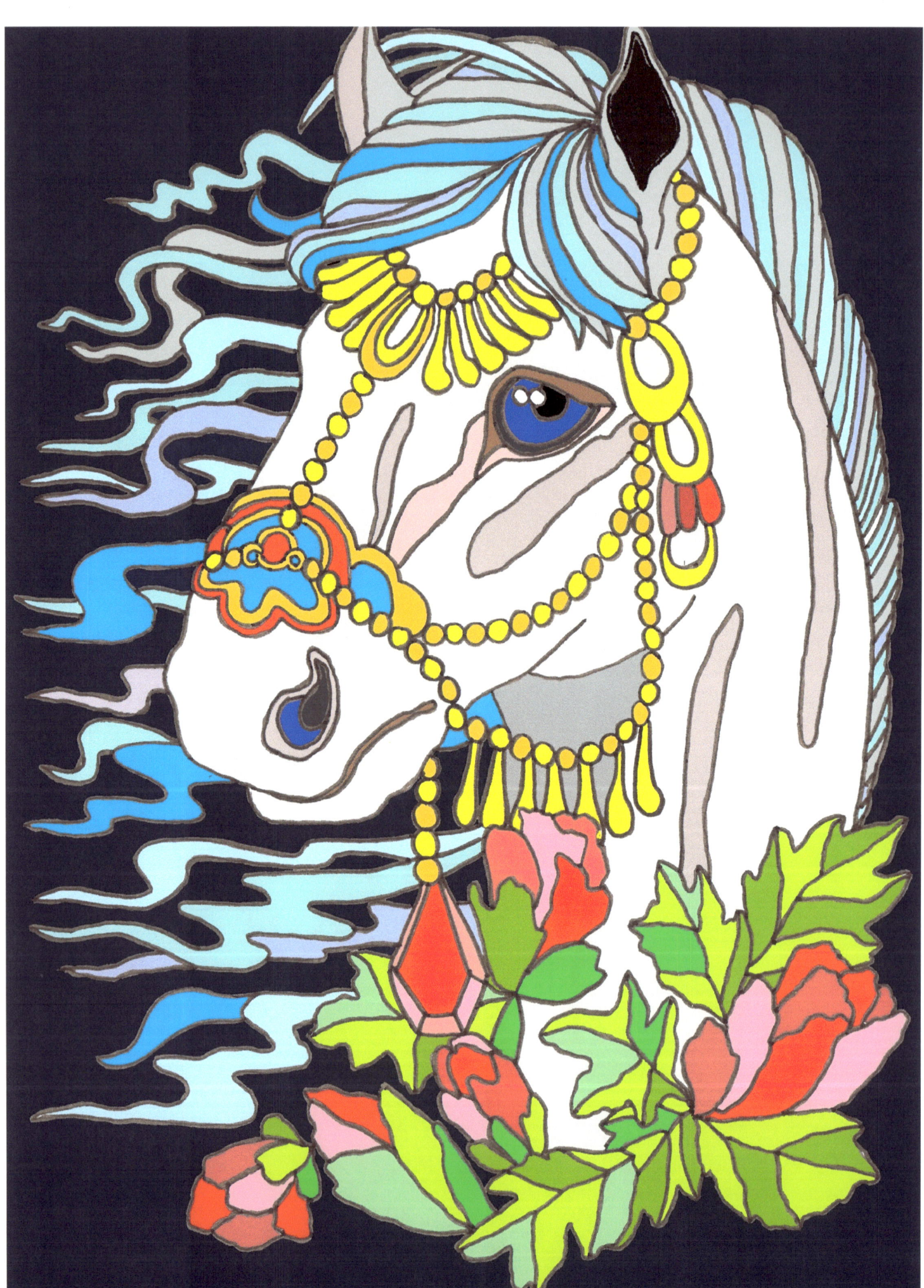

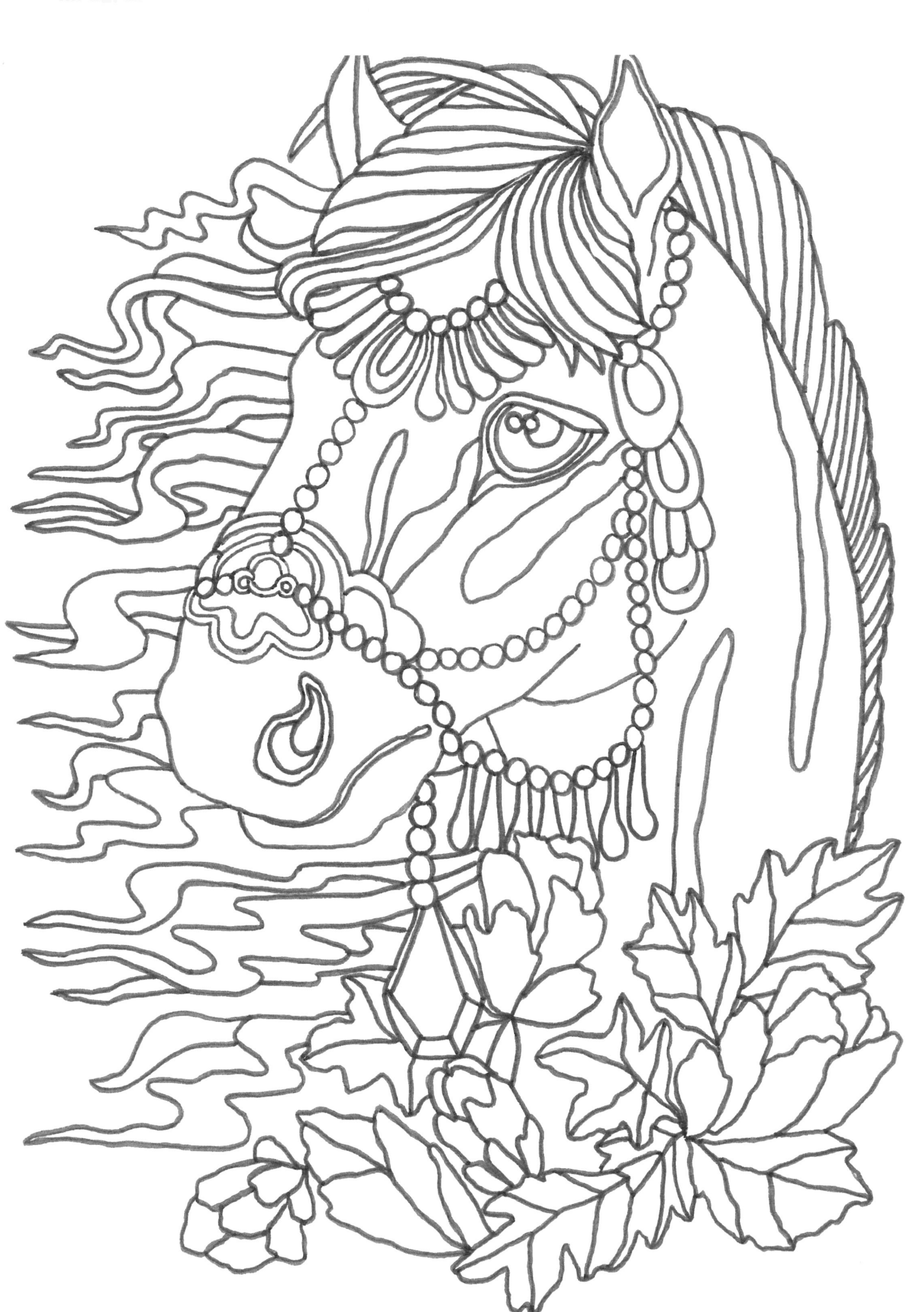

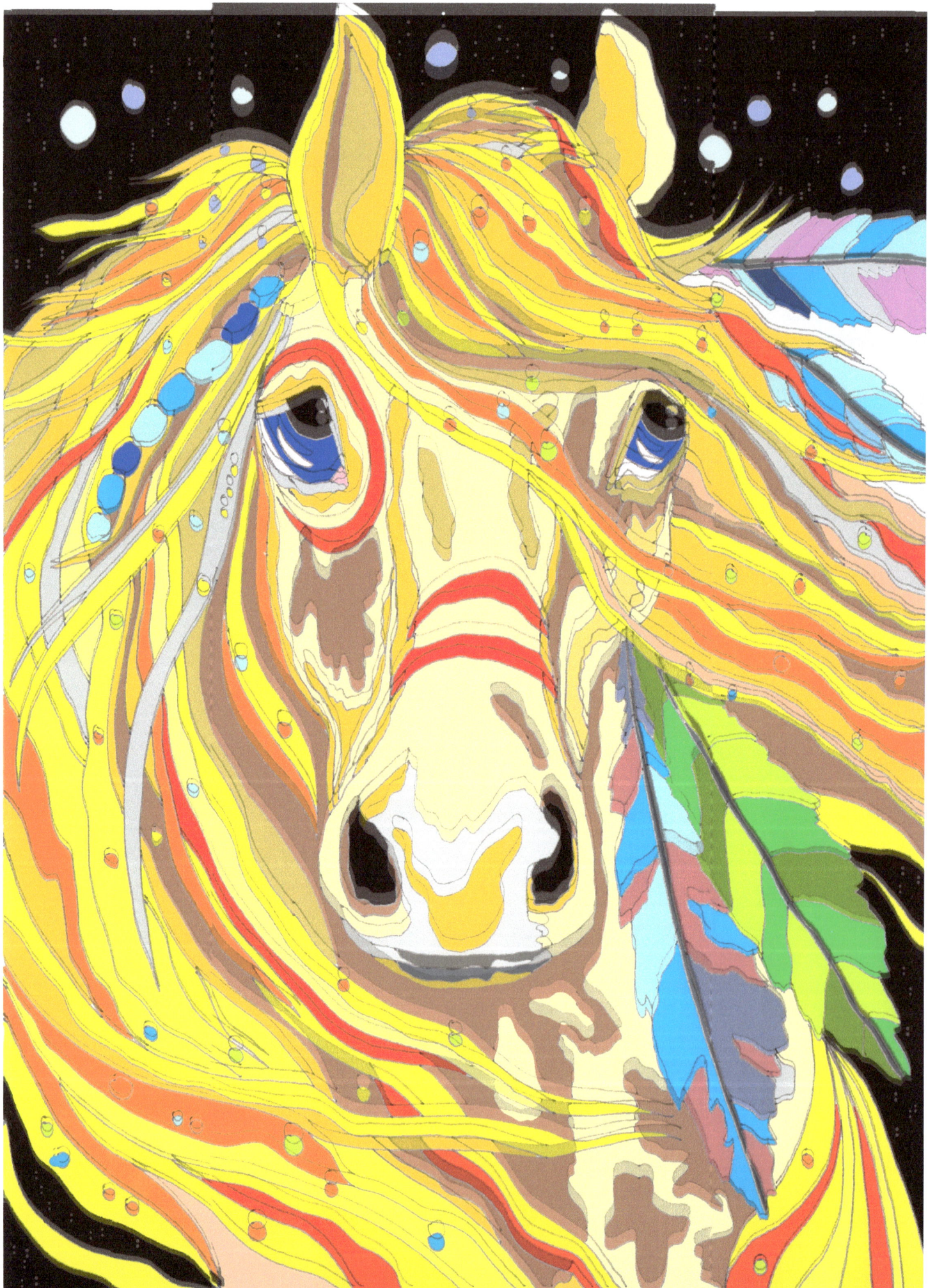

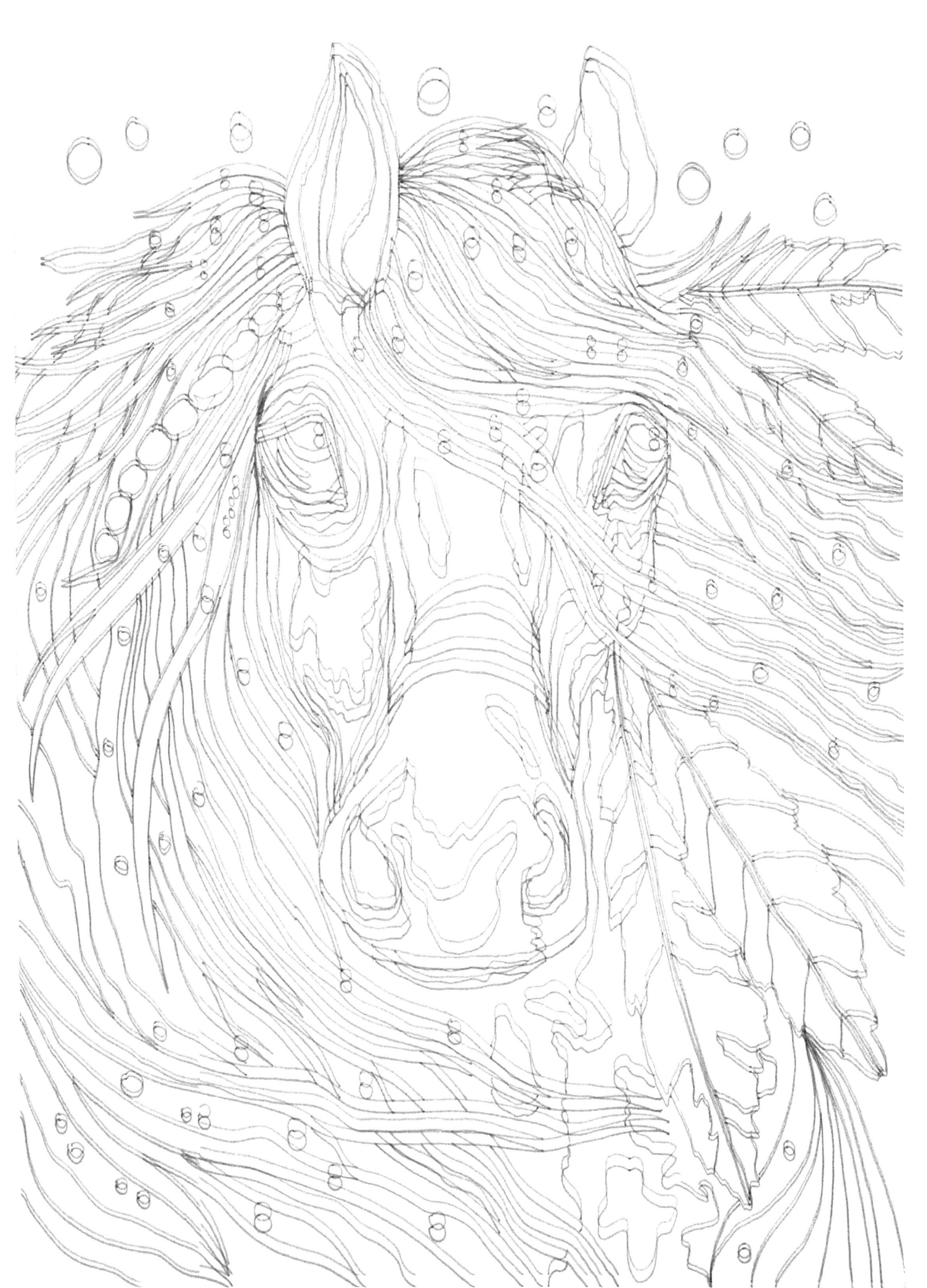

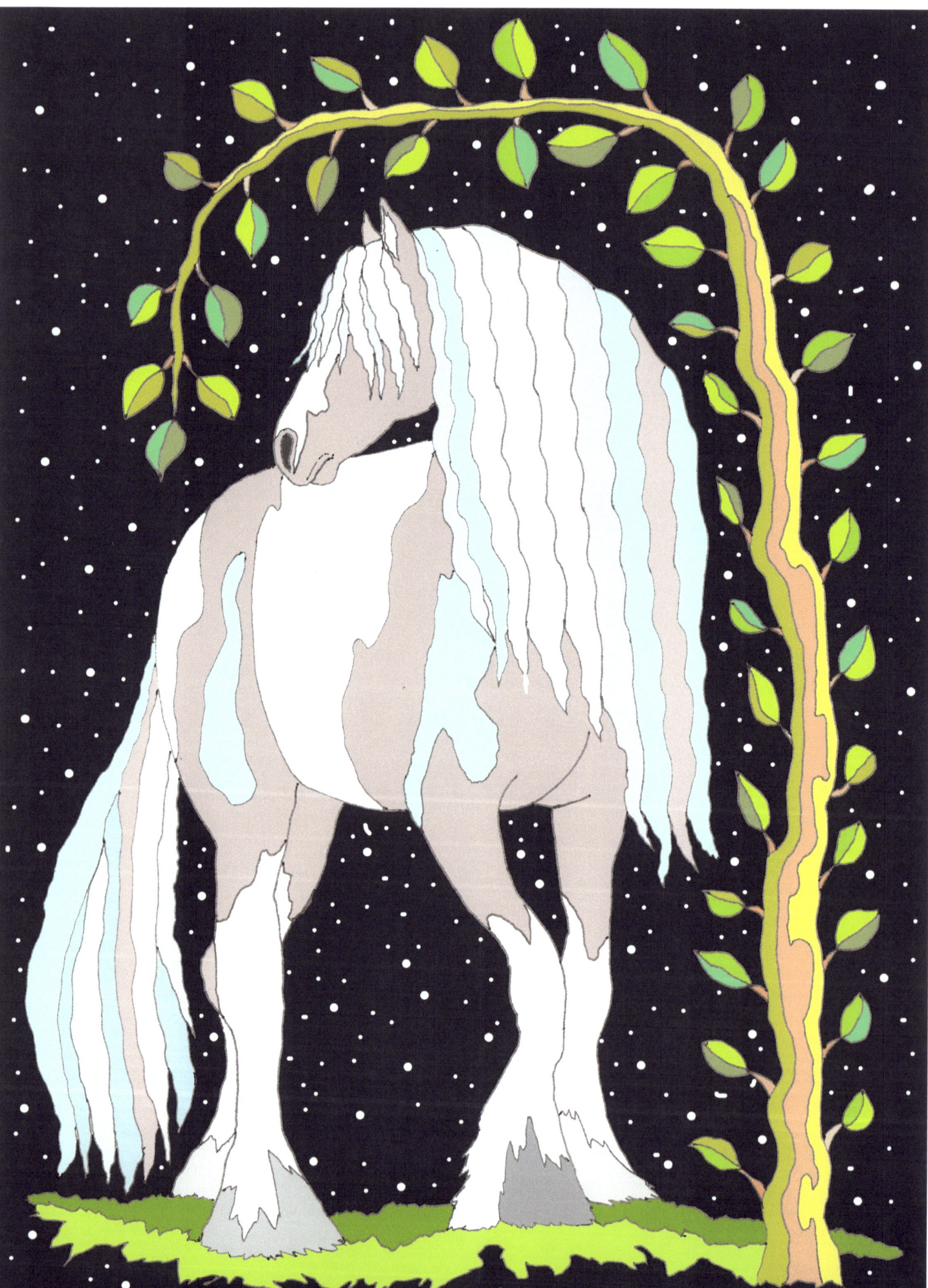

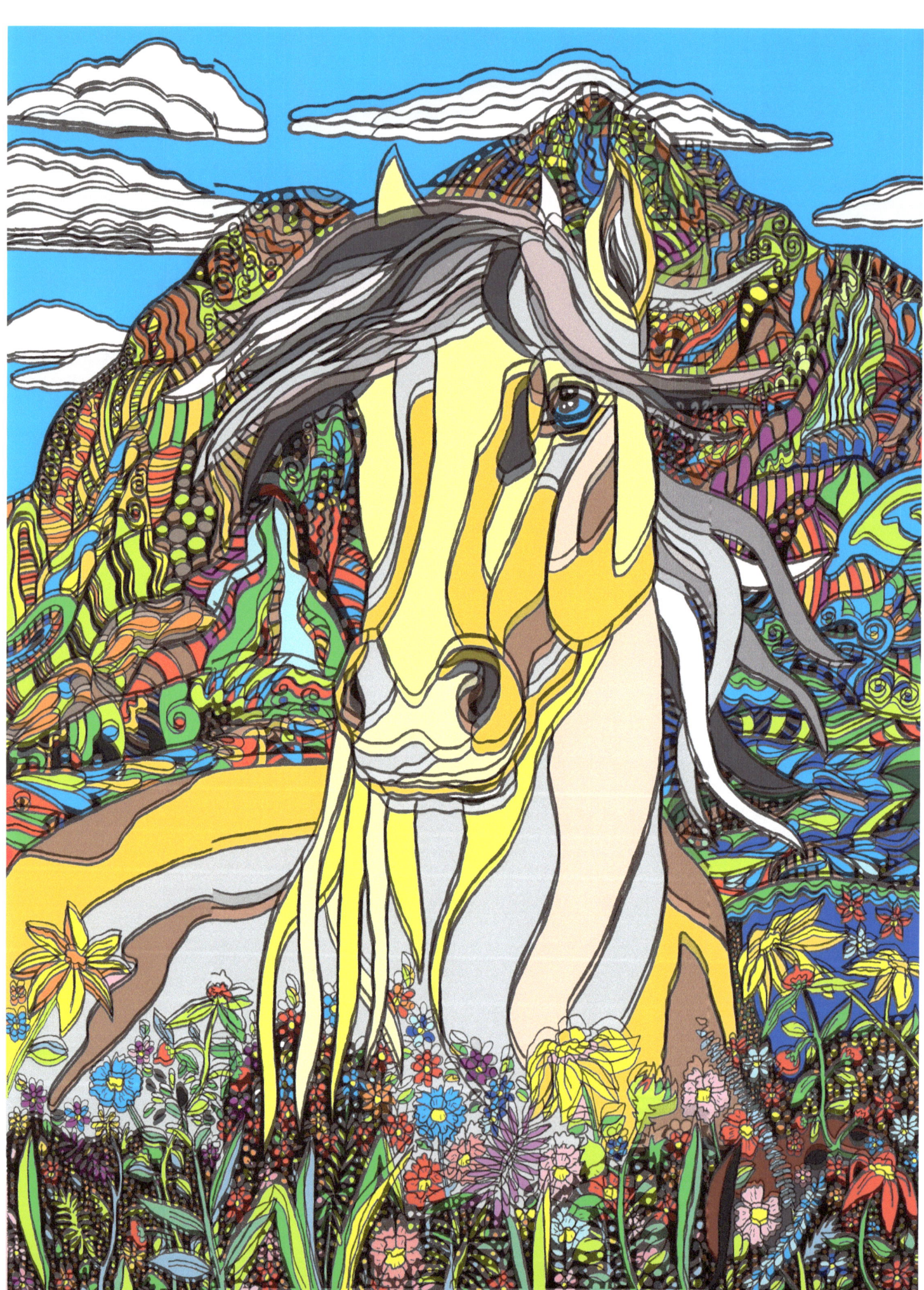

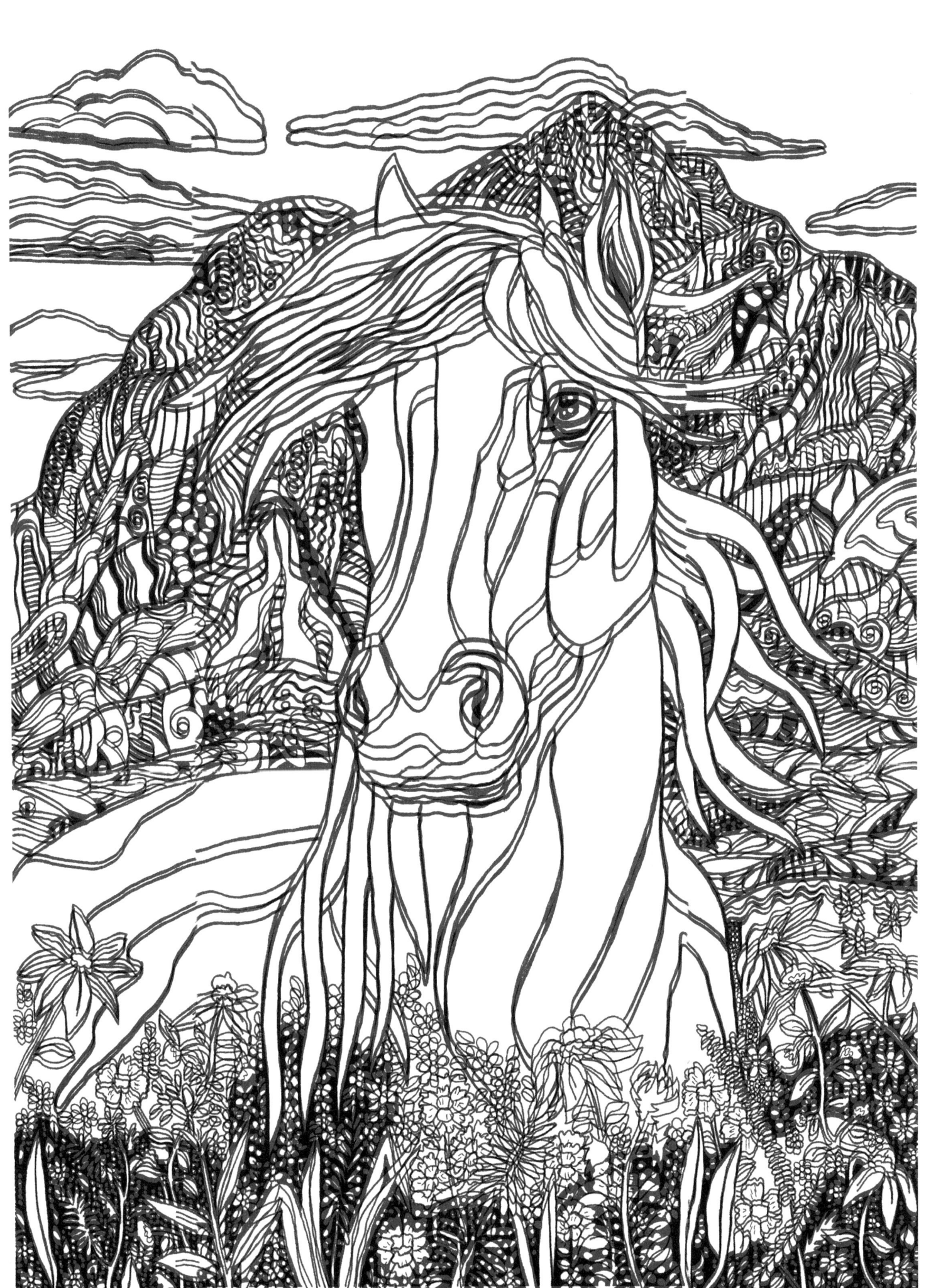

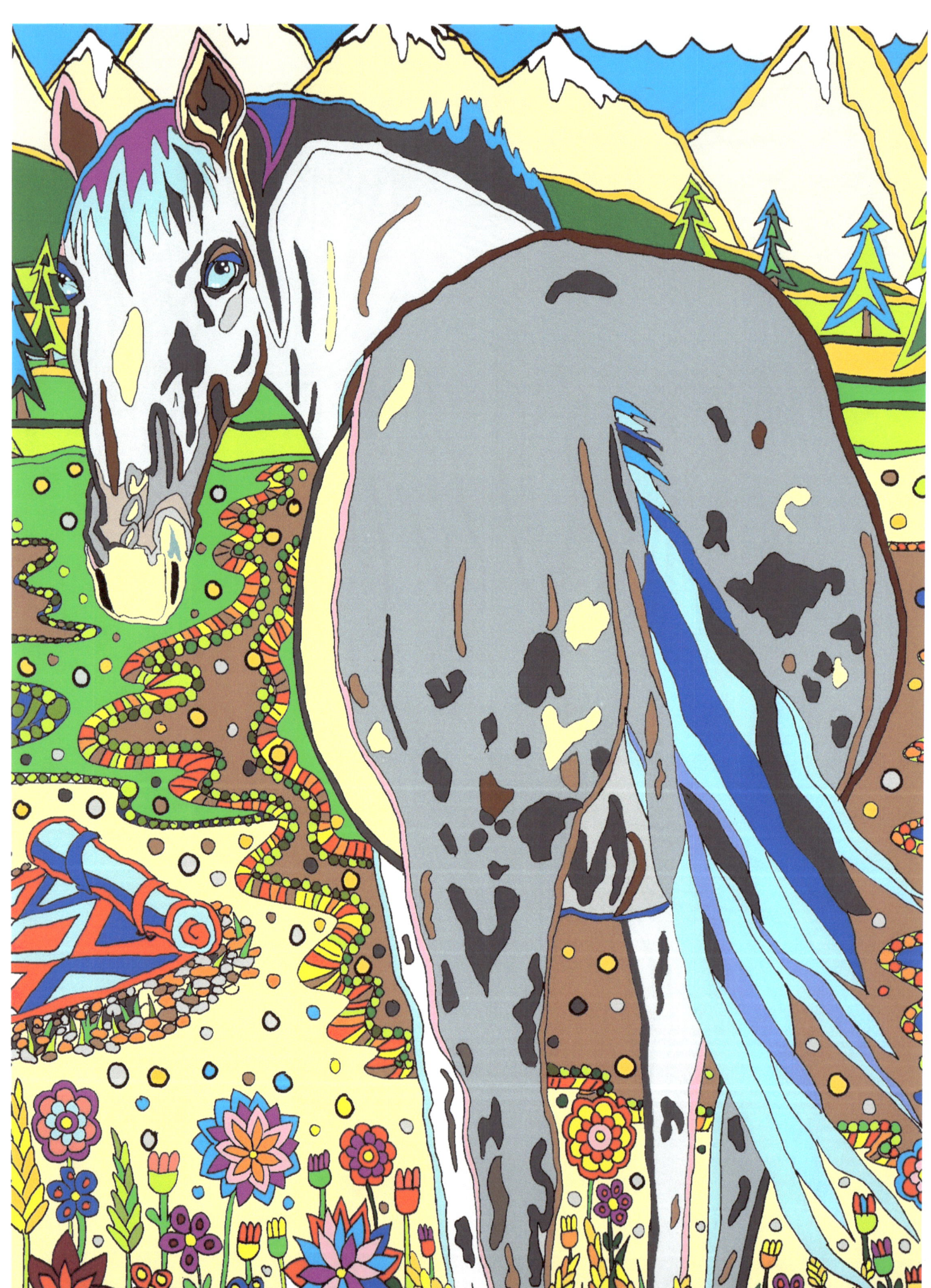

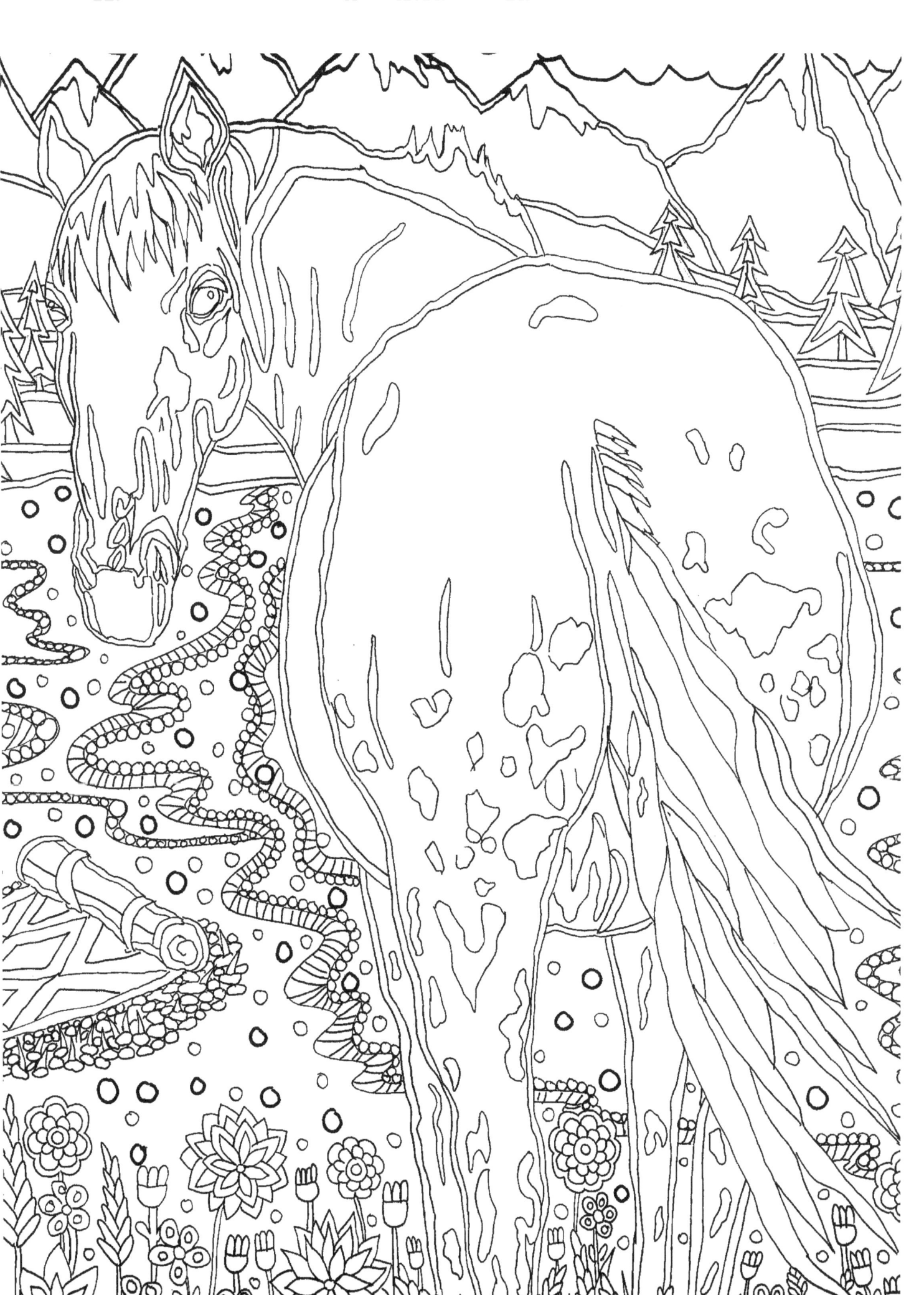

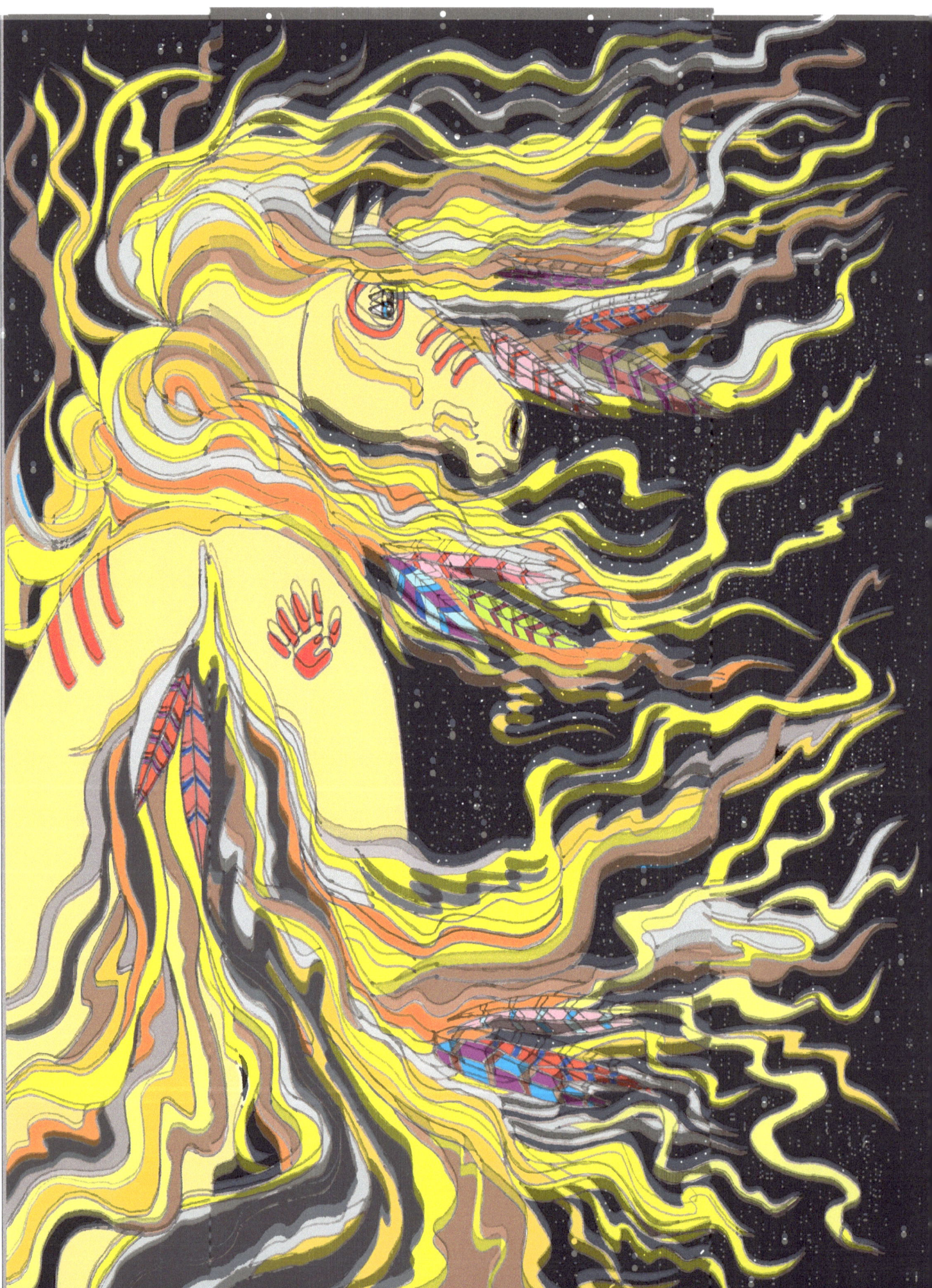

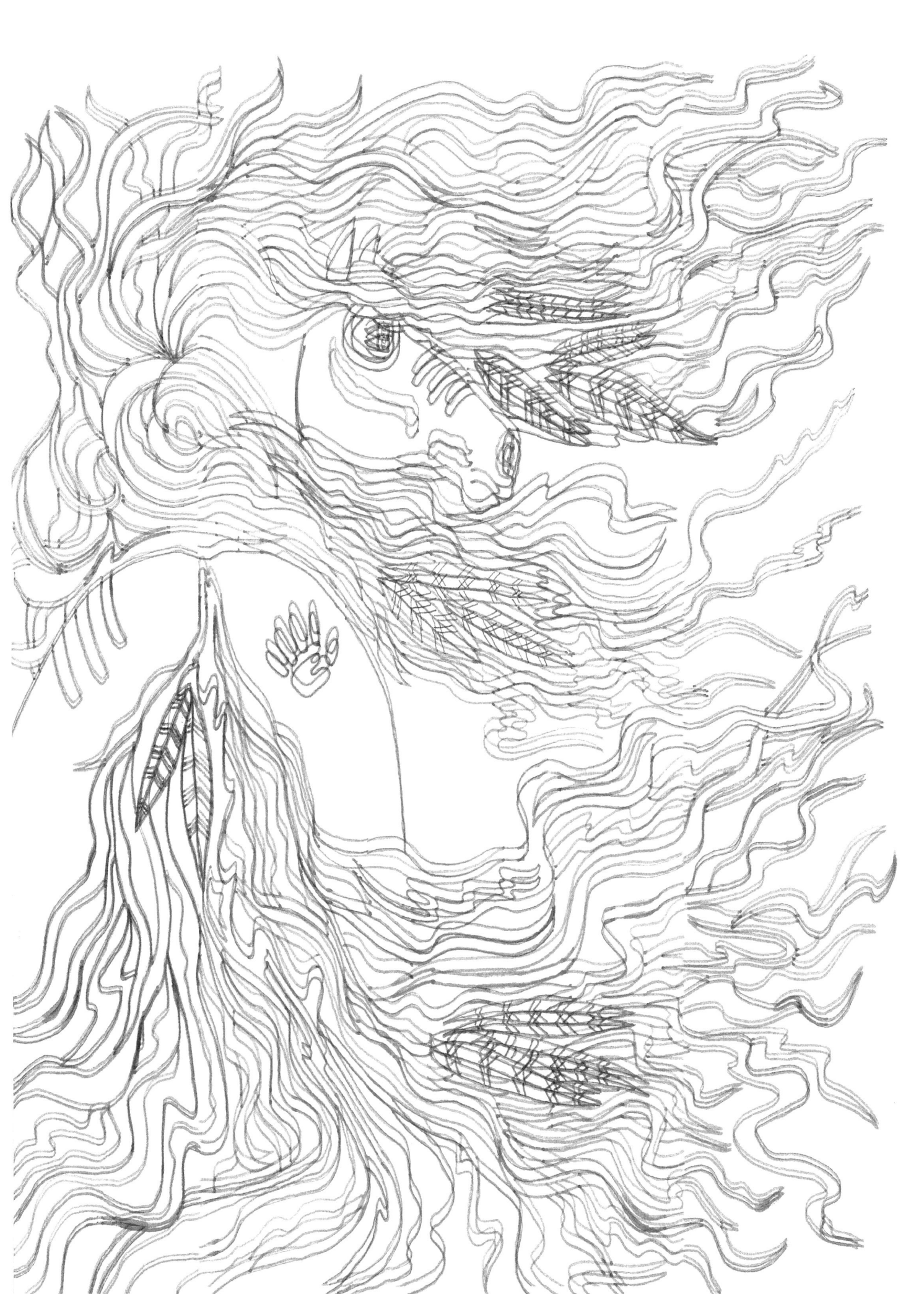

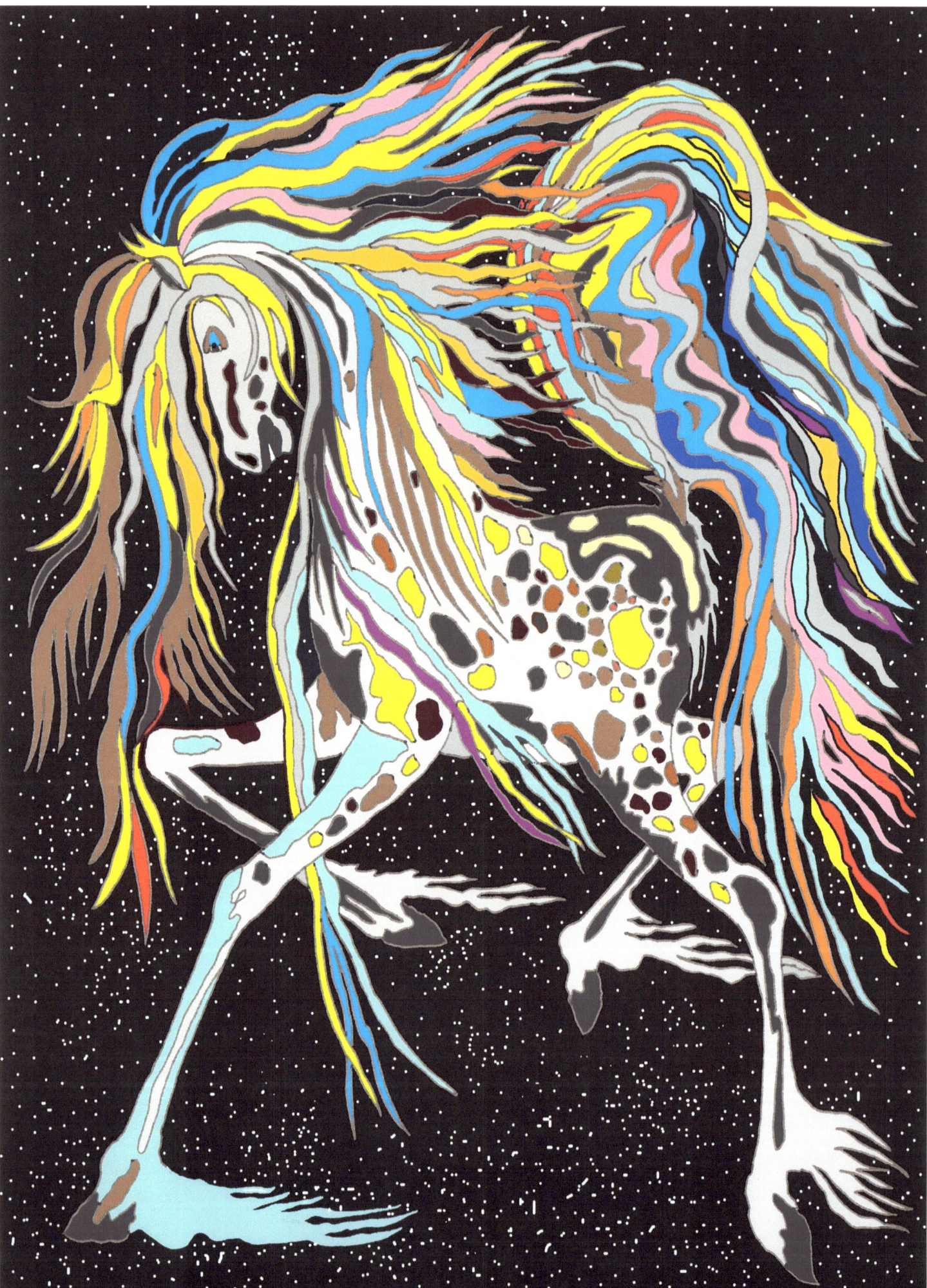